A DREAM HOUSE

Exploring the Literary Homes of England

by
Carol Chernega

First published by Dog Ear Publishing
4010 W. 86th Street, Ste H
Indianapolis, IN 46268
www.dogearpublishing.net

ISBN: 978-145750-246-0

This book is printed on acid-free paper.

Printed in the United States of America

This book is dedicated to
my husband John,
whose unfailing support and
encouragement kept me going.

ACKNOWLEDGMENT

Sincere thanks to the
Jane Austen Society of North America
(JASNA)
for offering the International Visitor
Program, without which this book
would not have been possible.

TABLE OF CONTENTS

INTRODUCTION

"[I]t is no frivolous curiosity that sends us to Dickens' house and Johnson's house and Carlyle's house and Keats's house. We know them from their houses—it would seem to be a fact that writers stamp themselves upon their possessions more indelibly than other people."

Virginia Woolf

O n my first trip to Bath, a friend and I visited the Jane Austen Centre. We'd both read *Pride and Prejudice* in high school. My teenage life hadn't had much in common with that of Elizabeth Bennet and the snobbish Mr. Darcy, and I had cavalierly dismissed Austen as being out of touch with my world. I had never dreamed that, 30 years later, Jane Austen would lead me down a long path that would have an unexpected impact on my life.

That day in Bath, as we opened the door of the Jane Austen Centre, we entered the Regency age. Displays of Regency costume, explanations of society and manners, and, of course, Austen's time in Bath were covered. Two of her novels were set in Bath, and the displays emphasized that.

Still, I was disappointed that the building that housed the centre was not actually located in one of the three houses Jane had lived in during her time in Bath. Like Virginia Woolf, I felt you'd truly know the writer if you knew the writer's home.

I decided I'd have to visit Austen's home, Chawton Cottage, on a future trip.

In the meantime, it was time to give Jane another chance. Upon returning home, I read *Sense and Sensibility* and loved it. I raced through all of her novels and then started on a biography.

One day, I saw a notice in the Pittsburgh newspaper about a JASNA (Jane Austen Society of North America) meeting that was taking place the following week. I went. I was warmly welcomed, but I immediately realized that I knew little about Jane compared to these people. I listened to them argue about what was wrong with the recent film adaptation of *Sense and Sensibility*, whether Marianne would really be happy with Colonel Brandon, and whether the film's Elinor lacked spunk worthy of an Austen heroine.

I was eager to learn more and continued to attend local meetings of JASNA. The following year I became President of the Western Pennsylvania region of JASNA.

By the time I finally visited Chawton Cottage, where Austen lived the last eight years of her life, I felt I knew her. Walking through the house where she had written her books and seeing the small bedroom that she had shared with her sister Cassandra helped me understand how her world had shaped her writing.

The following winter, I received my copy of the national JASNA newsletter, which announced the introduction of the International Visitor Program. I asked my husband, "What would you think of my going to live in England for two months, working for the Jane Austen Society?"

"Sounds good," he said immediately. (That's why we've been married so long.)

Three months later, I was chosen as the first International Visitor for JASNA. My responsibilities included working for the Jane Austen Society in Great Britain for two months, doing whatever they needed me to do.

My spare time was to be spent researching a literary project of my own. I proposed writing a book about the homes of English writers, which I originally saw as a travel guide, but as I traveled around England that summer, walking in the footsteps of my favorite authors, the book evolved into something more than a travel guide. It evolved into the book you hold in your hands.

Writers as diverse as Henry James and Agatha Christie referred to their homes as "dream houses." Many of the writers I discuss in this book used their homes as refuges for their writing. Some, like Agatha Christie and E. F. Benson, actually depicted their homes in their books. All of these created images that have remained vivid in readers' minds over the past two centuries because they were describing the towns and landscapes that they knew and loved.

The homes chosen to be covered in this guide had to meet two important criteria: First, they are all open to the public. Second, only writers who used setting as an important part of their work are included. Thus, Shakespeare, whose plays are focused mainly on character and plot, rather than on setting, is not included. (As the most visited writer's home in the world, Shakespeare's Birthplace hardly needs more publicity!) Sadly, homes of writers such as Daphne duMaurier, who definitely used setting as an integral part of her writing, are not included, as none of her homes are open to the public.

Please note that visiting times, policies, and admission fees change, and homes are occasionally closed for repairs, remodeling, or special events so do check in by phone or web site to avoid disappointment.

Most houses have a 'last admission time' policy which closes admissions about one hour before official closing time.

When calling from outside the U.K. dial your country's international access code (from the U.S. it's 011) then the U.K. country code (44) then the phone number (dropping the initial 0.) When calling from inside the U.K. you usually use the initial 0, unless you're within the area code that you're dialing.

All prices are given in British pounds.

A note on buses and trains: All buses and trains in England

run on the military clock. Thus, 8:00 refers to eight in the morning. Eight in the evening is referred to as 20:00. If traveling one way, ask for a single ticket. If returning the same day, ask for a same-day return ticket. Traveling by train after 9:00 a.m. will usually provide the best rate.

For good information on public transportation, check www.traveline.org.uk for suggested routes. For train schedules go to www.nationalrail.co.uk and for the London Underground check www.tfl.gov.uk.

Many thanks are due to the curators and librarians of the homes covered, who cheerfully gave of their time to help me understand the importance of the collections in each home.

Chapter One

JANE AUSTEN'S HOUSE MUSEUM

Home of Jane Austen, 1809–1817

[T]hey were wise enough to be contented with the house as it was; and each of them was busy in arranging their particular concerns and endeavoring, by placing around them their books and other possessions, to form themselves a home.

Jane Austen, *Sense and Sensibility*

*B*ack in the late 19th century, a man named Octo owned a tuck shop (sweets shop) in the city of Winchester. One day, he stopped a woman in the street named Mrs. Dick and said, "Excuse me. Could you please put a sign on my building that says Jane Austen died here?"

"Why do you want me to do that, Octo?" asked Mrs. Dick.

5

"Well, the Americans come in, and they want to know did Jane Austen die here, and they take up my time, and they don't buy anything!"

So, in due course, the first sign was placed on the house at 8 College Street that said Jane Austen died there in 1817.

Several months later, Octo saw Mrs. Dick again. "Please, could you take down that sign?" he pleaded.

"Why, Octo?"

"Well, the English people see it, and they come in, and they want to know, Who is Jane Austen?"

I'm happy to report that the English people now do know who Jane Austen is, as I'm sure many of them did back then. That's mainly due to the enduring quality of Austen's writing. But it's also due to the efforts of the Jane Austen Society and the Jane Austen Memorial Trust, two groups that formed back in the 1940s for the purpose of buying and preserving Chawton Cottage, Jane's home during the last eight years of her life.

Interest in the society spread around the world, and JASNA (Jane Austen Society of North America) was formed in 1977. JASNA selected me as their first International Visitor, sending me to Chawton to work for two months in the summer of 2005. The purpose of the International Visitor Program is to foster greater communication between the Jane Austen Society and JASNA.

I would be living in Winchester for the summer, the city where Jane had been sent for treatment when she had become ill. The treatment failed, and, as Octo was to learn, Jane died in Winchester and was buried in Winchester Cathedral.

On a previous visit to England, I'd visited Jane's grave in the cathedral and spent an afternoon at Chawton Cottage. But now I would be an insider, working for the Jane Austen Society three days a week. One day would be spent at the Chawton House Library, a recently opened library devoted to early women's literature. Another day, I would work on transcribing the early minutes of the Jane Austen Society. The Society members wanted to get these handwritten minutes onto a computer disk so the records would be safely preserved for the future.

Because I was a gardener by profession, it was decided that I would work one day a week with the gardener at Chawton Cottage. This was the assignment that most excited me. Before I'd left home, I'd told anyone who would listen, "I'm going to work in Jane Austen's garden!"

As I took the bus from Winchester to the village of Chawton, I felt nervous but excited. I'd be walking in the same places where Jane had walked. I'd be working to make her garden a place that visitors would enjoy. In my tote bag was a pair of brand-new gardening gloves, ready for weeding or pruning or whatever was required.

Celia Simpson, Chawton's gardener, welcomed me at the garden gate and took me on a tour of the garden. Underneath Celia's polite manner, I sensed I was being tested. Was I knowledgeable enough to work in Jane's garden?

"Do you know what this plant is?" Celia asked several times during the tour. Luckily, I was able to identify most of the plants. Whenever I couldn't identify something, I'd excuse my lack of knowledge by saying, "Oh, we don't grow that in Pennsylvania. It's too cold." Luckily, I didn't have to fall back on this excuse too often.

Celia explained that not much was known about the specific plants or layout of the garden during Austen's time at Chawton, other than from a few references in her letters and in the memoirs of people who visited the Austens. The garden layout that visitors see today was commissioned by the Jane Austen Society back in 1959. It has several elements of typical cottage gardens: hedges as walls, a cutting garden that was out of sight of the general public, colorful herbaceous borders, and several wooden benches to provide comfortable seating areas.

When she first started working at Chawton, Celia had decided that she would grow only plants that would have been known in Austen's day, creating a garden that would be authentic to the early 19th century. This created one problem for me: digging out dandelions. Or, rather, *not* digging out dandelions. Because dandelions might have been used in Austen's time for food or medicinal purposes, the dandelions were left to go their merry way. As a professional gardener, I would normally pull out any dandelion I saw without even thinking twice, so it was a real struggle to leave the dandelions intact. Occasionally, I would find a dandelion growing right up through another "good" plant and I would appeal to Celia. "It really has to go or it will choke out the good plant," I'd argue.

Celia would smile indulgently. "Go ahead," she'd say. It became a running joke with us by the end of the summer. But I also found it was helpful when I returned home. When visitors raised eyebrows at the sight of dandelions in my garden, I'd say airily, "If they're good enough for Jane Austen's garden, they're good enough for mine."

Working side by side with an English gardener was a wonderful way to immerse myself in the British attitude toward gardening. For instance, the British add a delightful sense of whimsy to their gardens. Celia dug out two small ferns and pushed them under a couple of slates on the kitchen roof. The ferns thrived in the damp shade provided by a yew tree, the only tree surviving at the cottage from when Austen lived there.

One day, Celia found one of the ferns lying on the ground under the yew tree. She surmised that it had suffered from "finger blight," a disease well known to gardeners at historic homes. A visitor had probably wanted to take home a little bit of Jane Austen's garden and had plucked the fern off the roof and left it under the tree until the person was ready to leave, then either forgot it or perhaps wasn't able to retrieve it without being seen. In any case, Celia re-planted the fern, a little higher on the roof this time, so it wasn't as easily susceptible to finger blight.

Another difference between American and British gardeners is that the British are much more committed to composting than are American gardeners. Celia and I composted everything in three large purpose-made bins. Invasive weeds and large branches that couldn't be composted were burned once or twice a year so that nothing went to landfills. Small sticks, instead of being composted, were used for staking plants that needed support, like climbing sweet peas or top-heavy hollyhocks.

British gardeners also have a more realistic acceptance of what they have to work with. The soil in this area is very chalky, so Celia had learned over the years which plants adapted well to chalky soil. I think American gardeners would try to change the soil so they could grow acid-loving plants like hydrangeas and rhododendrons, but that is so rarely successful that it's not worth the effort.

I also learned the value of elevenses. At eleven o'clock, we'd stop and have tea in the garden. The staff from the house would come out and join us when they could. Unlike the break I'd usually take back home, when I'd gulp down bottled water and rush back to work, at Chawton Cottage we would make ourselves comfortable on one of the garden benches and sit and talk for half an hour. At first, I found myself impatient to get back to work, but as the summer wore on, I realized that taking a longer break gave me more energy for getting my work done the rest of the day.

One day, while I was planting some liatris in the cutting garden, a voice behind me said, "Excuse me, are you Carol Chernega?"

I turned, startled. I knew nobody in England besides the people at the cottage. Straightening up, I saw a blond man with twinkling eyes standing behind me. "I just wanted to thank you for taking care of my aunt's garden," he said.

Thinking he was related to a client back home, I frowned, wondering who it could be. Then it dawned on me that Jane Austen was the aunt.

The man introduced himself as Patrick Stokes, a descendant of Jane's brother Charles. As we chatted, I tried to imagine how I could work this into a casual conversation back home. *Oh, yes*, I'd say, *I met a relative of Jane Austen's.*

Patrick asked if I would help set up for the AGM, or annual general meeting, of the Jane Austen Society. He'd need me for the setup on Friday, and the meeting would take place Saturday.

On Friday afternoon I worked with Patrick and several other volunteers on the grounds of the Chawton Library. The conversation centered on the question of what to give the speaker the next day. A woman would have been given flowers, but this speaker was male, so flowers didn't seem quite right. Several ideas were tossed around, but finally Patrick said, "Oh, I'll just give him an acorn from Aunt Jane's oak tree."

I laughed to myself at that dry British sense of humor, but the next day, I discovered that there were, indeed, acorns from Aunt Jane's oak tree.

The story goes that Jane Austen planted an oak tree at Chawton Cottage. Sadly, several years ago, this tree died. Just outside the brick wall to the side of the house, however, there was a small oak tree, presumably a descendant from the one Austen had planted. Celia had moved this tree inside the garden to protect it. When the old oak tree was cut down, pieces of it had been sent to a carpenter, who carved little acorns from the wood. It was one of these acorns that was given to the speaker the next day. And I can tell you that everyone in the audience wished they were being given an acorn from Aunt Jane's tree.

Born in 1775, Jane Austen lived most of her life in the county of Hampshire. The seventh of eight children, Austen was taught by her father, Reverend George Austen, the rector of Steventon. A prosperous, forward-thinking man, he encouraged Jane's love of reading and writing. Growing up in a rectory had its influence in her later writings. Every Austen novel has a clergyman character, sometimes sympathetic (like Edward Ferrars in *Sense and Sensibility*), sometimes buffoonish (like Mr. Collins in *Pride and Prejudice*).

In 1801, when George Austen retired, he moved the family to Bath, where they lived for five years. By most accounts, Jane was not very happy in Bath. In Jane's novel *Persuasion*, Anne Elliot's opinion of Bath is generally thought to mirror Jane's: "Anne disliked Bath, and did not think it agreed with her." Even when a character seems to be complimenting the city, the reader senses Jane's underlying satirical tone. Mrs. Allen says, "Bath is a charming place, sir; there are so many good shops here … one can step out of doors and get a thing in five minutes."

After Reverend Austen's death, Jane, her mother, and her sister, Cassandra, moved to various locations for several years but longed for the countryside. When Jane's brother Edward offered his mother and sisters the cottage at Chawton, they quickly accepted.

This two-story 17th-century brick building seems more like a manor house than a cottage. Five chimneys punctuate the steeply pitched roof, while two dormer windows add character to the otherwise plain façade. Chawton Cottage was part of the 265-acre Chawton Manor Estate, which Edward owned. The story of how Edward came to own this estate is a rather unusual one.

A distant cousin and his wife had no children to inherit their estate, so they asked Jane's parents if they could adopt the Austen's son. After much thought, the decision was made, and the couple formally adopted Edward. When the cousin died, the terms of the will dictated that Edward change his last name from Austen to Knight. This is how he came to inherit the Chawton Manor Estate, along with Godmersham in Kent.

The theme that women could not inherit estates or titles is one that runs through many of Austen's novels. This is why, in *Sense and Sensibility*, the Dashwoods must move out of the family home. Their half-brother inherits the estate when their father dies, forcing them to leave. Although their new home is a good size, much like Chawton Cottage, the Dashwoods are dismayed at their reduced circumstances. The Dashwoods are in such dire straits that they can have only three servants in the new household.

One can't help but wonder how Jane Austen felt about accepting her brother's largesse. A recurring theme in Austen's novels is the social standing of unmarried women and their reliance on the kindness of others. The Dashwoods' new home, for example, is actually owned by a cousin. However Austen may have felt about living on her brother's estate, her letters confirm that much visiting was done between Chawton Cottage and Chawton House, just as the characters in her novels fill their days with visits to friends and relatives. In fact, Austen admired her brother's home, Chawton House, so much that she may have used it as the inspiration for Mr. Knightley's manor home described in *Emma*.

Family loyalty is another major theme running through Austen's novels. In both *Sense and Sensibility* and *Pride and Prejudice*, loyalty between sisters is an essential element of the story. This loyalty is mirrored in Jane's own life. She was devoted to

Cassandra and was very fond of her brothers as well as of her nieces and nephews.

The most important aspect of Chawton Cottage is that, while living there, Jane Austen finally fulfilled her dream of publishing her work. *Sense and Sensibility*, which had been started several years earlier, was revised and published in 1811. In addition, Jane revised and published *Pride and Prejudice*, previously titled *First Impressions*. She also wrote *Emma*, *Mansfield Park*, and *Persuasion* while living at Chawton. The latter was published posthumously, along with *Northanger Abbey*, which had been written earlier. Her books were never published under her own name during her lifetime. *Sense and Sensibility* was modestly attributed, "By a Lady." *Pride and Prejudice* was referred to as "by the author of *Sense and Sensibility*."

Since her death, however, Jane's six finished novels have rarely been out of print. Details of village life may have changed over the past two centuries, but Jane Austen's stories of life and love contain universal truths, which still resonate with readers. Another major theme of her books is the virtue of country life versus the vice of city life. Visiting Jane's last home and walking through the villages of Chawton and Alton gives one a glimpse into that simple country life, when family loyalty and neighborly concern were unquestioned principles. Pleasures like walking in the country and playing the piano for guests were the highlights of the day. Like Elizabeth Bennet in *Pride and Prejudice*, Jane walked through the countryside almost daily, convinced that fresh air was good for her.

VISITING JANE AUSTEN'S HOUSE MUSEUM

Administered by the Jane Austen Memorial Trust
Village of Chawton, one mile southwest of Alton
Hampshire
Phone: (0)1420 83262
www.jane-austens-house-museum.org.uk/
Hours: September 1 - January 1, daily 10:30 a.m.–4:30 p.m.
    (Closed December 25 & 26)

January 2 - February 28, weekends only; 10:30
a.m.–4:30 p.m.
March 1 - May 31, daily 10:30 a.m.–4:30 p.m.
June 1 - August 31, daily 10:00 a.m.–5:00 p.m.
Admission: adults £7.00; concessions to seniors and children
Groups have a discount rate but must book in advance.
The curator or education director can give a short talk to
interested groups.
Wheelchair access: ground floor, garden, toilets
Large, lovely gift shop.

Upon arrival, pay the admission fee in the old granary. Follow the signs to the other side of the house and enter the recently renovated kitchen. Kitchen accessories authentic to the period have been carefully placed in this room. Next, enter the parlor where Austen and her mother and sister would spend the evening. In this room are displays detailing the family history. The piano is not Austen's but is similar to the one she played every morning before breakfast. One of her music books, with her signature on the front, is hanging in a wall case. On the wall is a portrait of Fanny Knight, Edward's oldest daughter and Jane's favorite niece. The Hepplewhite bureau, bookcase, and chairs belonged to George Austen. The bookcase has several early editions of Austen's books.

The next room would have been used as a dining room. The dining table is set with Wedgwood china. One of Jane's letters to her sister describes the shopping trip with her brother when this china was purchased.

The most significant object in the room is her writing table, in the far corner near the fireplace. It's hard to imagine Austen writing her books or correcting manuscripts for the publisher on this little round table that is half the size of today's average end table. The table seems laughably small compared to the huge complexes we now need for our computers, printers, and other writing paraphernalia. That she could compose her brilliant works with just a pen, paper, and this tiny desk is a humbling lesson to writers. Her folding writing desk (even smaller than this table) is now on display at the British Library in London.

Leave by the squeaking door to proceed upstairs. The story goes that Austen refused to allow the door's hinges to be oiled because the squeaking door gave her time to hide her writing from prying eyes. Nobody outside of the immediate family knew of her writing. She kept it hidden even from the servants.

On the stairway landing is a partial listing of the furnishings that the Austens sold when they left Steventon for Bath. It seems that almost everything they owned was sold, giving a hint of why the move to Bath was so traumatic for Jane.

Upstairs, Jane's bedroom is the first room on the left. Framed letters testify to the writer's legacy and popularity. One, from Sir Walter Scott, written after her death and lamenting her loss, shared the fact that he was reading *Pride and Prejudice* for the third time. A quote from Winston Churchill, taken from his book *World War II*, relates that his daughter Sarah read *Pride and Prejudice* to him while he was sick and claims that this reading helped to speed his recovery.

The next room was Jane's mother's bedroom. Here, information about Austen's brothers, as well as locks of Jane's hair and other relics, are on display. The fireplaces are original to the house, but none of the bedroom furniture actually belonged to the Austen family, although it's authentic to the period.

Along the hallway are dozens of framed illustrations from some of Austen's books. The first room on the right, probably a servant's room, contains pictures and information about all the places Jane lived during her short life.

The room at the end of the hall on the left has subdued lighting to protect the fabrics in the room. The prize display is a patchwork quilt made by Austen, her mother, and her sister, which has been meticulously restored. The design from this quilt was used by Laura Ashley to create a new wallpaper design. Two mannequins in the room are meant to represent Austen and her sister Cassandra arriving home from a formal party.

Outside, a visit to the bakehouse gives additional insight into the life of the Austen family. The bakehouse contains the huge copper kettle where water for the laundry would have been heated. It also has on display the donkey cart used by Jane near the end of her life when she was too ill to walk.

The old granery is now a lovely gift shop and is a treasure trove of all things Jane Austen, including new and second-hand copies of her books. They also sell numerous biographies of Austen, as well as academic studies of her work. High quality tea sets, bookmarks, pens, and notepads, many illustrated with the sketch of Austen drawn by her sister, Cassandra, are also on sale. A recent product line has been added to the gift shop's offerings, featuring botanical illustrations based on photographs that the gardener, Celia, took in the garden. Some items in the gift shop are illustrated with a Jane Austen silhouette taken from a second-edition copy of *Mansfield Park*.

Finally, don't miss the garden. There are several benches scattered around the garden on which to relax and contemplate the impact Austen has had on literature. And if you see Celia working, tell her I said hello.

GETTING THERE

By train: From London: Take the train from Waterloo rail station to Alton. Then take a taxi, or take the #64 bus to Alton Butts. If taking the bus, you'll have about a 10-minute walk up the Winchester Road to reach Chawton Cottage.

By bus: From Winchester: Take the #64 bus to Alton or Guildford (roughly a 35-minute bus ride). Chawton is a request stop, so tell the bus driver you want to get off near Chawton. Then you'll have a 10-minute walk to Chawton Cottage.

By car: From M25 Junction 10, take the A3 Guildford Bypass. Then take the A31 Farnham and Alton Bypass. Turn off left at A31/A32 junction roundabout. A public parking lot is in back of the Greyfriar car park opposite the museum.

PLACES TO EAT

Excellent homemade light lunches and teas are available at Cassandra's Cup across from the house, open Wednesdays through Sundays.

Greyfriar Pub is also across from the house, open daily.

WORKS BY AUSTEN

Sense and Sensibility—1811
Pride and Prejudice—1813
Mansfield Park—1814
Emma—1816
Persuasion—1817
Northanger Abbey—1817
Lady Susan
The Watsons
Sanditon

RELATED SITES TO VISIT

CHAWTON HOUSE LIBRARY

Chawton
Alton, Hampshire GU34 1SJ
Phone: (0) 1420 541010
www.chawton.org
Wheelchair access: Ground floor only.

Chawton House was part of the estate owned by Jane Austen's brother Edward. Extensive renovations were done from 1995 to 2003 to restore the house and create a research library devoted to early women's writing. Those wishing to use the library must make an appointment in advance and fill out an application, available online.

Guided tours are now available of the house and library every Tuesday and Thursday from March through December, and Tuesdays only in January and February. Tours start at 2:30 p.m. Admission fee is £6.00 for adults, £3.00 for children. Tours are occasionally cancelled because of special events.

The garden is open for self-guided tours Monday through Friday from 10:00 a.m. to 4:00 p.m. Admission fee is £3.00. Pay in the office and collect a garden pamphlet.

Group tours, educational events, and space for weddings and conferences are also available. Check the web site or call the number above for details.

At the bottom of the driveway leading up to Chawton House is the church where Jane Austen's mother and sister are buried.

It's a 10-minute walk from Chawton Cottage to Chawton House Library. (Ask at the Cottage for directions.)

WINCHESTER CATHEDRAL
Winchester SO23 9LS
Phone: (0)1962 857200
www.winchester-cathedral.org.uk
Cathedral is open 9:00 a.m.–5:00 p.m. Mon.–Sat.; 12:30–3:00 Sundays
Free tours on the hour Monday through Saturday, 10:00 a.m.–3:00 p.m.
Specialized tours such as the Jane Austen Tour are also available. Call to book.
Audio tour (narrated by David Suchet) is available for £3.00
Evensong: 5:30 p.m. daily; 3:30 p.m. Sundays
Admission: £6.00; Children under 16 free
Wheelchair access: most parts of cathedral

Winchester Cathedral is the burial place of Jane Austen. Winchester was the capital of Saxon England and is about an hour's train ride southwest of London.

When Jane became ill in 1817, possibly with what is now known as Addison's disease, she and her sister, Cassandra, moved to Winchester to consult a doctor. The doctor couldn't help, and Jane died two months later at the age of 41. Two of her brothers carried her coffin to the cathedral, a building she greatly admired. She had made the arrangements for the burial upon moving to Winchester, so she had obviously known the end was near.

Austen's grave has been one of the most-visited spots within the cathedral since the late 1800s. The large gravestone set in the floor commemorates the "benevolence of her heart, the extraordinary endowments of her mind." Nearby, on the north wall, hangs a tall brass memorial plaque that was installed in 1872. By then, Jane was well known; the plaque refers to her writings. In the gallery, there's a silhouette of Austen circa

1815, which is inscribed on the back: "Jane Austen done by herself." A special Jane Austen exhibit is underway.

Guided tours of the cathedral are available by volunteer guides and are worth taking.

After visiting the cathedral, exit through The Close onto Kingsgate Street. Turn left onto College Street. On the right, at number 8 College Street, you'll find a discreet plaque by the door identifying this cottage as the place where Jane Austen died. This is now privately owned, so do not disturb the residents.

GETTING THERE

By train: One hour from London Waterloo. At the Winchester train station, take the #5 bus to the City Centre. There's a Tourist Information Centre at the train station and also one at the Guildhall in the City Centre.

Alternatively, from the train station, walk the roughly half mile into town. From the train station, turn right onto Station Road, then left onto Upper High Street. It is claimed to be the oldest street in any English city, dating back 2500 years. The centerpiece of Winchester is the statue of King Alfred the Great, who ruled Wessex from 871 to 899. Just past the statue, follow the signs to the cathedral.

PLACES TO EAT IN WINCHESTER

Near the cathedral, the Refectory Café, run by volunteers, provides good home-cooked lunches and tea. Not open for dinner, and lunch service stops at 2:30, but teas are available the rest of the afternoon.

Café behind Guildhall: Hot entrees plus good salads.

Forte Brasserie and Tea Rooms: at 78 Parchment Street. Serves breakfast until 11:30 a.m., light lunches and dinners such as jacket potatoes, Ploughman's, or pasta; plus cream teas.

BATH
Jane Austen Centre
40 Gay Street; Queen Square
Bath BA1 2NT
Phone: (0)12254 43000

www.janeausten.co.uk
Hours: March 26 – October 30: 9:45 – 5:30 daily
      late closing July and August 7:00 p.m. Thursday – Saturday
      November 1 – March 25 Sunday – Friday: 11:00 a.m. – 4:30 p.m.
      Closed December 24 – 26 and January 1
Admission: £7.45 Concessions for seniors, children and families
Wheelchair access: ground floor only
Gift shop.

Jane Austen and her family moved to Bath in 1801 when her father, Reverend George Austen, retired. From most accounts, she wasn't very happy in Bath and did little writing during the five years she lived there. Still, *Persuasion* and *Northanger Abbey* are set there, and they perfectly capture the social whirl prevalent in Bath in the early 1800s. The Pump Room was obviously the place to see and be seen, as described in *Northanger Abbey*: "Every morning now brought its regular duties... the Pump Room to be attended, where they paraded up and down for an hour." Balls took place in the Assembly Rooms, then called the Upper Rooms. Austen would have attended these, as she loved to dance. Again in *Northanger Abbey*, she says: "The season was full, the room crowded, and the two ladies squeezed in as well they could. As for Mr. Allen, he repaired directly to the card-room, and left them to enjoy a mob by themselves."

Austen lived in four houses in Bath, but one was destroyed during WWII, and the other three are privately owned and not open to the public. The Jane Austen Centre, however, can be visited. Set in an elegant 1750s home in Gay Street, the centre presents an authentic period atmosphere. With reproduction costumes and original maps and drawings of Bath, you can imagine you're strolling through early 19th century England. Gaze through bow-fronted shop windows typical of Austen's time, as well as recreations of Georgian parlors. Quotes from the novels and scenes from the recent films are sprinkled throughout the displays, reminding visitors of Austen's lasting appeal.

Letters were the main form of communication in the 1800s, and Austen wrote many, especially to her sister, Cassandra. Copies of some of her letters are on display here, as are first editions of her books. Two large displays focus on her background, on how and where she was raised and on an extensive family tree. The centre also presents a complete bibliography of her published work, as well as notable events in her life. You can even get a photograph of yourself taken in period costume.

GETTING THERE

By train: London Paddington to Bath Spa. From the Bath train station, head for the abbey, where there's a Tourist Information Centre. Here you can pick up a street map of Bath as well as buy tickets for a one-and-a-half-hour walking tour of Jane Austen's Bath, which starts at 11:00 am daily. Additional tours are conducted by Blue Badge Guides every Friday at 2:30 p.m. starting from the Jane Austen Centre.

LONDON

British Library: 96 Euston Road (www.bl.uk): Austen's handwritten manuscript of the *History of England*, written when she was 16, is on display, as well as her writing desk. Underground stop: Euston or King's Cross

National Portrait Gallery: St. Martin's Place (www.npg.org.uk): View the pencil-and-watercolor portrait of Austen drawn by her sister, Cassandra. Underground stop: Charing Cross

Westminster Abbey: (www.westminster-abbey.org): Visit the memorial to Jane Austen. Underground stop: Westminster

ARMCHAIR TRAVELING

www.goucher.edu/library/austen_home.htm Goucher College in Baltimore, Maryland has an extensive Jane Austen collection.

www.jasna.org is the web site of the Jane Austen Society of North America.

www.janeaustensociety.org.uk is the web site of the Jane Austen Society of the U.K.

www.pemberley.com is a fun web site for Austen fans. It's named for Mr. Darcy's estate in *Pride and Prejudice*. It also links to dozens of other Austen web sites.

FURTHER READING

A Memoir of Jane Austen: and Other Family Recollections by James Edward Austen-Leigh

A Portrait of Jane Austen by David Cecil

Jane Austen A Life by Claire Tomalin

Jane Austen for Dummies by Joan Klingel Ray

Chapter Two

Wordsworth House, Dove Cottage, and Rydal Mount

Homes of William Wordsworth

**Wordsworth House 1770 – 1783
Dove Cottage 1799 – 1808
Rydal Mount 1813 - 1850**

*Where once the DOVE and OLIVE-BOUGH
Offered a greeting of good ale
To all who entered Grasmere Vale;
And called on him who must depart
To leave it with a jovial heart;
There, where the DOVE and OLIVE-BOUGH
Once hung, a Poet harbours now,
A simple water-drinking Bard*

Wordsworth, *The Waggoner*

*V*isiting these three homes in the order in which Wordsworth lived in them effectively illustrates the changes in Wordsworth's life. Start with the solid-looking Wordsworth House, in the center of the town of Cockermouth, where he was born on April 7, 1770. Here he passed the first few years of his life in relative comfort and security, with his mother and father, sister, and three brothers. After the early death of their parents, the children were sent to various homes, dependent on relatives and strangers for their support.

Next, visit the picturesque but cramped Dove Cottage, into which William and his sister, Dorothy, moved in 1799. Here, Wordsworth wrote most of his best work and began achieving fame as a poet. As he married and began having children, the size of the cottage would become increasingly inadequate. In 1813, the family would move to Rydal Mount, Wordsworth's home for the last 37 years of his life. On top of the mountain, both figuratively and literally, Wordsworth enjoyed at Rydal Mount a permanent view of the source of much of his poetic inspiration: his beloved Lake District.

When his mother died in 1779, William and one of his brothers were sent to live with a woman named Ann Tyson, in Hawkshead, a small town near Windermere. Tyson had become like a second mother to William, and he visited her frequently after leaving her household.

William's father died in 1783, and problems with his father's will meant the children were destitute. William and his three brothers and their sister, Dorothy, were sent to live with their uncle. They were not especially welcomed into the house and consequently were not treated well.

School offered a way out. In 1787 William attended Cambridge, intending to become a lawyer like his father. He disliked the school, however, and although he received his degree, he decided to go to France to study language. This was at the beginning of the French Revolution, and Wordsworth met people on both sides, all of whom influenced his ideas on politics and religion. He also met a young woman named Marie Anne Vallon (sometimes called Annette), with whom he fell in love. Although Wordsworth and Annette had a daughter together, they never married because of her parents' objections, and Wordsworth eventually returned to England.

Although he toyed with the idea of entering the clergy, William ultimately gave up this plan and dedicated himself to writing poetry. A small legacy enabled William and his sister, Dorothy, who was devoted to him, to rent a house in southwestern England. Here he met Samuel Taylor Coleridge for the first time, and thus began a long friendship.

Coleridge and Wordsworth decided to write a book together, which was published as *Lyrical Ballads* in 1798. This book is widely considered to mark the beginning of the Romantic Age of poetry, and Wordsworth and Coleridge were the major players in this movement.

The main theme of the Romantics was an appreciation for the beauty of nature and man's relationship to it. This coincided with several developments in the arts. Up until the early 1700s, artists mainly painted people. When landscapes were included in a painting, man was usually shown as commanding or improving the land. In the 1700s, however, landscapes began to be painted for their own beauty, with man receding into the background for a sense of perspective, or sometimes to animate the view.

At the same time, landscape designers were extolling the virtues of the Picturesque style of design. They proposed that garden views should be designed to imitate the viewpoint of a painting.

These changes all coincided with improvements in roads and traveling conditions in rural England. The Lake District, with its mountainous backdrop, became a prime tourist destination. Written travel guides began appearing, many of which promoted Picturesque touring. These guides used poetry and paintings to illustrate what travelers could expect to experience.

Wanting to share his love of the beauty of the lakes and the mountains, Wordsworth wrote *A Guide to the Lakes* in 1810. This travel guide was a bit too successful in bringing people to the area. The crowds that resulted from this promotion of his beloved landscape dismayed Wordsworth.

Wordsworth loved to walk, and in 1790, he took the first of a series of walking tours, this one through France and Switzerland. His account of this trip, *Descriptive Sketches of a Pedestrian Tour in the Alps*, was published in 1793.

In 1799, William and Dorothy moved into Dove Cottage, a house they had long admired, near the village of Grasmere. The cottage was originally an inn called the Dove and Olive, immortalized in Wordsworth's *The Waggoner*.

Soon after moving in, William was off on another of his rambling walks. While he was gone, Dorothy decided to write a journal, now referred to as the *Grasmere Journals*, which she thought he would enjoy reading when he returned. In the journal, she not only described her daily activities but also recorded her observations of the countryside. This was the beginning of one of the best creative collaborations in English literature. Dorothy's writings were never published during her lifetime but have since been shown to be the inspiration for many of William's poems.

After seeing a field of daffodils near the lake, for example, Dorothy described the experience: "Under the boughs of the trees, we saw that there was a long belt of them along the shore. . . . They grew among the mossy stones about and about them; some rested their heads upon these stones as on a pillow for weariness; and the rest tossed and reeled and danced."

Wordsworth's poem "The Daffodils" begins

> I wandered lonely as a cloud
> That floats on high o'er vales and hills,
> When all at once I saw a crowd,
> A host, of golden daffodils;
> Beside the lake, beneath the trees,
> Fluttering and dancing in the breeze.

Although Wordsworth later credited his wife, Mary, with suggesting the first two lines of the poem, the inspiration was clearly taken from Dorothy's description.

This was the most prolific period of Wordsworth's work, and many of his most popular poems were written while he lived at Dove Cottage. He also began writing a long piece that reflected his experiences from childhood, through school at

Cambridge, to his experiences in France. It was an ambitious attempt to trace the development of his mind by tracing his development as a human being. This manuscript, titled *The Prelude*, is now considered his masterpiece, although it wasn't published until after his death.

While living in Dove Cottage, Wordsworth married a childhood friend, Mary Hutchinson, and they had five children. They preferred to live simply and economically, a fact noted by Sir Walter Scott, who reported that when he visited the Wordsworths, two of the three daily meals he was served were porridge.

The Wordsworths hosted numerous friends at Dove Cottage, such as Charles and Mary Lamb, Samuel Taylor Coleridge, and Poet Laureate Robert Southey, who lived nearby. The cottage was becoming too small for the growing family and all of their visitors, so William and Mary's family moved, living in two other houses before finally settling in Rydal Mount. Mary's sister and Dorothy both moved with them. Around this time, Wordsworth was made Distributor of Stamps for the county of Westmorland, which gave him enough income to rent this larger house.

Life at Rydal Mount continued much as before, although Wordsworth wrote less. He enjoyed working in his garden and also designed gardens for friends. Wordsworth is said to have claimed that if he hadn't been a poet, he would have been a gardener.

Upon the death of Robert Southey, a request came from the queen for Wordsworth to fill the post of Poet Laureate. Actually, what sounded like a request was really a command, and Wordsworth rather daringly refused. When pressed, Wordsworth replied that at his advancing age, he didn't feel up to writing any official verse, which would be required by the person holding this position. When assured that he wouldn't have to do so, he accepted the position. He was rather proud of the fact that he never did write any official verse.

Wordsworth died on April 23, 1850, the same date as Shakespeare's birth and death. He's buried in the Church of St. Oswald in Grasmere.

VISITING WORDSWORTH HOUSE

Administered by the National Trust.

Main Street

Cockermouth, Cumbria CA13 9RX

Phone: (0)1900 820884

www.wordsworthhouse.org.uk

Hours: Open late March through late October (exact date
varies annually)
Saturday to Thursday, 11:00 a.m.–5:00 p.m.
Closed Fridays

Admission: Adults £6.20; concessions to children and families
Reduced rate is available when arriving by public transportation. Show travel ticket before paying.

Group rates available, including an introductory talk
(advance booking is essential)

Wheelchair access: to ground floor only

Entry is on a timed ticket, so buy tickets first, then wander around the town if you have a long wait before entering the house.

Costumed guides demonstrate what life was like during Wordsworth's time. Hands-on activities are available for children.

GETTING THERE

By train – Workington station is 6 1/2 miles away. Then take a taxi, or bus as below.

By bus – from Workington train station: 35/6 Workington to Cockermouth.

Or: Stagecoach in Cumbria X4/5 Penwirth to Workington via Keswick.

All buses stop on Main Street.

By car – Follow the A595 to A5086 to Cockermouth. Follow brown signs to Wordsworth House

Or: follow the A66 to A5086 to Cockermouth

Or: follow the B5295 (Lorton Road) to Cockermouth

Car parking in the town center car parks

VISITING DOVE COTTAGE

Administered by the Wordsworth Trust.

Grasmere

Cumbria LA22 9SH

Phone: (0)1900 824805

www.wordsworth.org.uk

Hours: November 1 –February 28 9:30 a.m.–4:30 p.m. daily
      March 1–October 31, 9:30 a.m.–5:30 p.m. daily
      Closed December 24–26 and most of January (varies
      annually)

Admission: Adults £7.50; Concessions to children and families

Group rates available but must book in advance

Admission price includes a visit to the Wordsworth Museum and Art Gallery next door.

Joint ticket with Rydal Mount is available.

Wheelchair access: Dove Cottage, ground floor only; Wordsworth Museum fully accessible with ramps and lifts – the museum also has a virtual tour of Dove Cottage

Because the cottage is small, visitors are on a timed-entry system. A guided tour of the house is available.

The house is preserved much as it was when Wordsworth lived there from 1799 to 1808, giving visitors a good sense of what life was like for his family. Most of the furniture belonged to him. Personal possessions such as his ice skates are also on display.

The view from the front of the house now looks over a sheep farm, but in Wordsworth's time, the view to the lake would have been uninterrupted.

The parlor was probably the main bar when the house was the Olive and Bough. Gorgeous carved oak paneling surrounds the fireplace, and the floor is covered in local slate. The ceilings in this room and throughout the cottage are only seven feet high, making the cottage seem even smaller than it is.

The downstairs bedroom was first used by Dorothy, later by William and Mary. Their rare double washstand is an interesting feature of the room. The three oldest children, John, Dora, and Thomas, were born in this room.

The kitchen is simple by today's standards but apparently served the Wordsworths' simple needs perfectly. The stone-walled larder is next to the kitchen, which has a delightful spring that helps to maintain a cool, even temperature year round.

Halfway up the staircase is a door to the garden. At the top of the stairs is Wordsworth's cuckoo clock, which still works.

Wordsworth did much of his writing in the sitting room. In addition to "The Prelude," many of his most famous poems, such as "The Daffodils" and "Ode: Intimations on Immortality," were written while he lived in this cottage. His unusual writing chair took the place of a desk. He would also entertain friends and take tea in this room.

When William married, Dorothy moved into the bedroom next to the sitting room. Next to it is the pantry, or lumber room, which would also have been used as a guest room. Off of that room is the Newspaper Room, so called because the Wordsworths papered it with newspapers. These newspapers were replaced in the 1970s, but with papers dating to Wordsworth's time, so visitors can read the news of that time.

GETTING THERE

Dove Cottage is located just outside the village of Grasmere on the A591, the Kendal-Keswick Road through the central Lake District.

By train: The Windermere train station is 8 miles away. Check at the Tourist Information Centre at the train station for information on the special tourist bus that stops near Rydal Mount and near Dove Cottage. Local buses are also available from the train station: #555 and #599.

By car: From the M6 exit at Junction 36, follow the signs for Kendal, Windermere and Ambleside to Dove Cottage.

VISITING RYDAL MOUNT

Ambleside
Lake District LA22 9LU
Phone: (0)15394 33002
www.rydalmount.co.uk

Hours: March 1–October 31, daily 9:30 a.m.–5:00 p.m.
November, December and February: Wednesday –
Sunday, 11:00 a.m.–4:00 p.m.
Closed December 25 and 26 and through January
Admission: adults £6.50; Concessions to families, students
and seniors.
Garden admission only: £4.00
Special group tours available but must be booked in
advance.

Rydal Mount was bought by Wordsworth's great-great-granddaughter in 1969 and has been open to the public since 1970. The family still uses the house occasionally, so only parts of the house are open.

The dining room was part of a smaller house dating back to the 16th century. Candlesticks in the dining room were carved from a yew tree planted by Wordsworth in Grasmere churchyard in 1819. A portrait of Robert Burns, Wordsworth's favorite poet and, according to him, his biggest influence, hangs in the dining room. A painting of Wordsworth by B. R. Haydon is also on display, the original of which is now hanging in the National Portrait Gallery in London.

The library and drawing room are spacious and decorated in a comfortable style with many of the Wordsworth family furnishings. Framed photographs are clustered on tables, and pillows are thrown onto chairs with an abandon that suggests that the family just stepped out. The only known portrait of Dorothy hangs above the fireplace in the drawing room.

Three bedrooms on the first floor are open. They belonged to Dorothy, William and Mary, and their daughter Dora.

On the second floor, Wordsworth's study has a magnificent view of the countryside. Many of his manuscripts and books are on display.

The grounds have been left much as William and Dorothy landscaped them, although the mature trees across the countryside now block what must have been a fantastic view of Lake Windermere. Still, this is one of my favorite gardens in England.

Various paths lead to wonderful views of the countryside and to Rydal Water, the smallest lake in the Lake District. In keeping with his views as a Romantic poet, Wordsworth thought that a garden should be informal and should blend into the natural landscape rather than fight it.

It's said that a servant once said to a visitor: "This is my master's library, where he keeps his books. His study is out of doors."

The terrace steps are said to have been laid by Wordsworth and lead, via the sloping terrace, to a slate and wood summerhouse. Called, appropriately enough, the Poet's Summerhouse, this was also built by Wordsworth.

If you are walking back to the bus stop, the best way to go is by way of Dora's Field. Planted with hundreds (now thousands) of daffodils in honor of his daughter Dora—whose death at age 43 left Wordsworth and his wife, Mary, desolate—this land is now owned by the National Trust. Once you have left Rydal Mount for Dora's Field, however, you cannot return to Rydal Mount, as a one-way gate prohibits reentry, but the field makes a lovely walk through the woodland, especially in the spring when the daffodils are blooming. The path comes out at Rydal Church, which has a lovely small garden.

GETTING THERE

Rydal Mount is 1 1/2 miles from Ambleside on the A591 Grasmere Road. See directions to Dove Cottage for nearest train station and buses.

WORKS BY WORDSWORTH

Lyrical Ballads—1798
Poems in Two Volumes—1807
The Excursion—1814
Ecclesiastical Sketches—1822
The Prelude—1850

RELATED SITES TO VISIT

THE WORDSWORTH TRUST (www.wordsworth. org.uk): Located in an old coaching house next to Dove Cottage, the Trust displays manuscripts, memorabilia, and paintings of Wordsworth, his family, and friends. Open 9:30 a.m.–5:30 p.m.

PARISH CHURCH OF ST. OSWALD, Grasmere: Wordsworth is buried here.

GRASMERE GINGERBREAD SHOP: Established 1854. Wordsworth liked the gingerbread from this shop in Grasmere Village. They make the same gingerbread today from a secret recipe, as well as a delicious rum butter.

ARMCHAIR TRAVELING

www.visitcumbria.com

www.cumbria.gov.uk suggests public transportation routes.

www.cumbria-tourist-board.co.uk

www.bu.edu/editinst/resources/wordsworth/index.html web site for the Wordsworth Circle, which discusses Wordsworth, Keats, and Austen; link to the Wordsworth-Coleridge Association.

FURTHER READING

William Wordsworth by Hunter Davies, 1997

Home at Grasmere, edited by Colette Clark, 1960. Presents William's poems alongside Dorothy's journal entries, effectively illustrating the inspiration Wordsworth got from her writings.

Chapter Three

HILL TOP

Home and studio of Beatrix Potter, 1905–1943

But don't go into Mr. McGregor's garden.

Beatrix Potter, *The Tale of Peter Rabbit*

From an early age, Helen Beatrix Potter was encouraged to paint and draw. Although she and her younger brother, Bertram, grew up in London, the Potter children loved nature. They smuggled small animals, such as mice, chipmunks, and frogs, into the house to play with and draw. During their summer vacations, first spent in Scotland and later in the Lake District, they took long walks in the countryside. This exposure to the beauty of northern Britain was to be an important influence on Potter's life and work.

Informally educated by a governess, Beatrix spent many days visiting museums near her home. The Natural History Museum was a special favorite, with its insect collections, which Beatrix spent hours sketching. The Victoria and Albert Museum, then known as the South Kensington Museum, also provided inspiration with its costume and furniture collections. A gentleman's waistcoat from the 1780s was later to become the inspiration for the mayor's wedding outfit in *The Tailor of Gloucester*.

Long into adulthood, Beatrix and her brother spent holidays with their parents, and when Beatrix was 29, they went to Sawrey in the Lake District. Beatrix began to focus on drawing fungi that she found in the woods. Her detailed drawings are beautiful in themselves, in addition to being botanically correct. She loved the Lake District so much that she hated to return to London and vowed to return to the area. Her drawings of a little bunny named after her own pet rabbit, Peter Piper, made it possible for this dream to come true.

One day Beatrix learned that a young boy named Noel Moore, the son of her former governess, was ill. She sat down and wrote him a letter that told a story about four rabbits. She used her own pet rabbit, Peter Piper, for the illustrations.

During a holiday in the Lake District, she showed her drawings to a visitor named Hardwicke Rawnsley, who later became one of the founders of the National Trust. Rawnsley admired Potter's talent and encouraged her to try to publish her work.

She started by selling some of her drawings to a greeting card company. She also asked Noel Moore to return the Peter Rabbit letter so she could turn it into a real story. When six publishers rejected the story, Beatrix decided to publish it herself. The story then came to the attention of Frederick Warne & Co. who published it, beginning one of the most successful associations in the history of children's literature.

The Tale of Peter Rabbit was so popular that it was reprinted six times in the first year. Warne published several more of Potter's little tales, and Potter was very involved in the design of the books and their covers. She had definite opinions about how the books should look, and luckily, the publisher trusted her judgment.

During this time, Beatrix fell in love with, and became engaged to, her editor, Norman Warne. Her parents thought Warne was too working-class for their daughter and strongly objected to the engagement. They wanted Beatrix to stay home and take care of them in their old age. Sadly, before Beatrix and Norman could marry, he died suddenly.

Beatrix decided to find another way to establish her independence from her parents. With the royalties from her books, she bought Hill Top Farm in 1905 and added on to the 17th-century house so she could live there when visiting from London. This new project helped her tremendously in recovering from the sadness brought on by Warne's death, as well as in giving her inspiration for her work.

Although Beatrix had drawn Mr. McGregor's garden from a farm she'd visited in earlier days, many of her books after she moved to Hill Top Farm were inspired by places and events at Hill Top. *The Tale of Tom Kitten* is set in Hill Top's house and garden. A straying duck from the farm became the inspiration for *The Tale of Jemima Puddle-Duck;* the wife of the manager of Hill Top and their children are the basis for many of the pictures in the book. *The Tale of Samuel Whiskers* features the rats that at one point invaded Hill Top's house.

Potter continued to buy surrounding land. A local solicitor, William Heelis, watched for property sales for her, and they became friends. On October 15, 1913, she married Heelis, again defying her parents' wishes.

The couple moved into Castle Cottage, a farm Beatrix had bought that adjoined Hill Top, but she continued to use Hill Top as her studio and study. In addition, visitors were now arriving to see the home that had inspired their favorite children's books. Beatrix was flattered by the attention and welcomed them graciously. Many visitors came from America, and in 1927, an American publisher asked Potter to write a special book for the American public. Titled *The Fairy Caravan*, it was a series of short stories about a traveling circus. It featured animals from Hill Top and its neighboring farms but was also somewhat autobiographical. Feeling rather shy about this, Potter refused to allow the book to be published in England. It was not available in a British edition until nine years after her death.

Potter published only four more books after her marriage. Not only did her eyesight start to fail, making it difficult for her to draw, but she also discovered that she enjoyed farming. She had developed a passion for the breeding of Herdwick sheep, becoming the first woman president of the Herdwick Sheep Breeder's Association.

She worked hard to preserve the Lake District, believing, as her old friend Hardwicke Rawnsley did, that it was important to keep large estates intact and preserve old cottages. She became a supporter of the National Trust, both financially and vocally. In 1930 she bought a 4,000-acre estate and offered to sell half of it to the National Trust at the price she'd paid for it. They not only raised the money to buy it but asked Potter to manage it.

When Potter died on December 22, 1943, her ashes were spread over the Cambrian Fells, keeping her forever on the land that she loved. She left all of her property to her husband, with the understanding that it was all to go to the National Trust after his death. She also stipulated that the Herdwick sheep breeding should continue. The farms and cottages on the property were rented, but the house at Hill Top was opened to the public in 1946.

VISITING HILL TOP

Hill Top
New Sawrey, Hawkshead
Ambleside, Cumbria LA22 0LF
Phone: (0)15394 36269
www.nationaltrust.org.uk (Search for Hill Top)
Hours: Closed Fridays
          Open early February through March, 10:30 a.m. – 3:30 p.m.
          April and May, 10:30 a.m. – 4:30 p.m.
          June through September 1, 10:00 a.m. – 5:00 p.m.
          September through October 30, 10:30 a.m. – 4:30 p.m.
Shop and garden hours: similar to house hours, but shop and garden are also open on Fridays, and also open until December 23.

Admission: adults £7.00, concessions to children and families
Free to members of the National Trust.
Entry to garden and shop is free.
Groups must book in advance.
Wheelchair access: ground floor only. Limited accessible
parking.
Gift shop.

Hill Top house is rather small and cramped, and the hordes
of visitors have forced the National Trust to use a timed-entry
system. Because of the crowded conditions, it's best to avoid
visiting during the peak summer season if possible. A tiny re-
creation of Mr. McGregor's garden is fenced off so that thousands of trampling feet don't destroy it, as Peter Rabbit was so
intent on doing.

Visitors approach the house along a winding flagstone
pathway, flanked on both sides by a lush, overgrown perennial
garden. The scene seems vaguely familiar, and indeed, the path
and garden with the house in the distance are depicted in both
The Tale of Tom Kitten and *The Tale of Pigling Bland*.

Passing through the small covered doorway, visitors are
immediately immersed in the world of Beatrix Potter. Most of
the furnishings were originally owned by Potter or are close
matches to items she had in the house. In fact, Potter left
detailed instructions on where each item was to be placed in the
house after her death.

The most effective feature of the house tour is the display
of Beatrix Potter books in each room. Each book is open to a
page that contains an illustration that matches what's on display
in the house. This emphasizes how frequently Potter used her
home, furnishings, and the views from the windows as inspiration for her drawings. When is a hole in the floor interesting?
When it's the hole that the rats used in *The Tale of Samuel
Whiskers*.

The entrance hall features an oak longcase clock that is
illustrated in *The Tailor of Gloucester*. That book is open to the
page depicting the clock. The parlor contains the Potter family coat of arms as well as a teapot that is illustrated in *The Tale
of the Pie and the Patty-Pan*.

The staircase itself was used in many book illustrations. Halfway up, at the turn in the staircase, is another longcase clock, which is drawn in the same location in *The Tale of Samuel Whiskers*. On the top landing, one can almost see Samuel Whiskers pushing his rolling pin across the Oriental rug.

Upstairs, Beatrix Potter's study and writing room (which she called the New Room, because it was part of an extension she added to the house) is where the feeling of Potter's presence is strongest. Even after moving out of the house upon her marriage, she spent much of her writing time in this room. It's easy to imagine her sitting at her desk, gazing out of the window for inspiration.

Be sure to look through the window at the view of Stoney Lane winding up the hillside. Again, an open book depicts the same view, this one from *The Tale of Samuel Whiskers*. Large landscapes painted by Beatrix's brother, Bertram, are on display here. The room is furnished with an 18th-century bookcase, and an Edwardian game table is set up with a game of cards dealt as though the players have just stepped out.

In Potter's bedroom is an impressive seventh-century four-poster bed. Two of Potter's dolls are also on display, and it's thought that these were the models for Lucinda and Jane in *The Tale of Two Bad Mice*.

Beatrix Potter loved to collect things, and the Treasure Room is full of samples of her mementos. In addition to china and jewelry, the room contains a dollhouse. In the dollhouse are pieces of the doll-sized food that Tom Thumb and Hunca Munca stole in *The Tale of Two Bad Mice*.

The Sitting Room also contains china and antique furniture, as well as photos from Potter's childhood and paintings by a variety of artists.

GETTING THERE

Hill Top is two miles south of Hawkshead in the village of Near Sawrey.

By train: Windermere train station; then 4 1/2 miles via vehicle ferry or take bus

By bus: From Windermere train station, take the 'Stagecoach in Cumbria', bus #505, from Windermere towards

Coniston; change in Hawkshead to Near Sawrey. This bus runs from April to September only.

By ferry: From Bowness pier 3, there's a combination passenger ferry/bus ticket available. (It's the 'Stagecoach in Cumbria' bus # 525, which stops at Hill Top, and also goes into Hawkshead.) There's also an off-road footpath from the ferry stop – about 2 miles walk to Hill Top.

By car: Take the B5286 or the B5285 from Ambleside (6 miles). From Coniston, take the B5285 (7 miles).

PLACES TO EAT

The Tower Bank Arms pub is a short walk from Hill Top.

WORKS BY BEATRIX POTTER

Potter wrote 28 books, including 23 of her "tales." This is just a selection of them:

The Tale of Peter Rabbit—1902
The Tale of Squirrel Nutkin—1903
The Tailor of Gloucester—1903
The Tale of Two Bad Mice—1904
The Tale of Mrs. Tiggy-Winkle—1905
The Tale of Tom Kitten—1907
The Tale of Jemima Puddle-Duck—1908
The Tale of Ginger and Pickles—1909
The Tale of Mr. Tod—1912
The Tale of Pigling Bland—1913

RELATED SITES TO VISIT

Beatrix Potter Gallery:

Administered by the National Trust
Located in Hawkshead, about two miles from Hill Top.
Main Street
Hawkshead, Cumbria LA22 0NS
Phone: (0)15394 36355
www.nationaltrust.org.uk
Open times similar to Hill Top.
Admission: adults £4.60, concessions to children and families.

Formerly the solicitors' office of Beatrix Potter's husband, William Heelis, this 17th-century building was bequeathed to the National Trust after his death. Original artwork by Beatrix Potter is on display, as is some of the original furniture from the solicitor's office. Artifacts relating to Beatrix Potter's family are also featured. The winding streets of Hawkshead are the setting for *The Tale of Johnny Town-Mouse*.

World of Beatrix Potter Attraction, Bowness-on-Windermere (www.hop-skip-jump.com) Geared mostly to children, this charming attraction is set up with re-creations of scenes from Potter's tales. Lots of special events for children. Phone: (0) 844 504 1233

Victoria and Albert Museum, London (www.vam.ac.uk): This museum has the largest Beatrix Potter collection in the world, but most of it is available by special appointment only. The star of the collection is the Peter Rabbit Picture Letter, which was sent to Noel Moore on 4 September 1893, telling the Peter Rabbit story for the first time. Also on display is the waistcoat that inspired the *Tailor of Gloucester*.

The nearest underground stop is South Kensington on the Piccadilly, Circle, or District line.

ARMCHAIR TRAVELING
www.vam.ac.uk Victoria & Albert Museum.

FOR FURTHER READING
The Real World of Beatrix Potter by Elizabeth Battrick, 1986
Beatrix Potter's Art by Anne S. Hobbs, 1989
Beatrix Potter: Artist, Storyteller and Countrywoman by Judy Taylor, 1989

Chapter Four

THE WORLD OF JAMES HERRIOT

Home of Alf Wight (aka James Herriot), 1940–1953 and his veterinary office, 1940–1990

I got out of the car and sat on the springy grass as I have done on countless occasions since then. I was captivated, completely spellbound and I still am to this day.

James Herriot, *James Herriot's Yorkshire*

From the moment he left Scotland for the small town of Thirsk in 1940, Alf Wight fell in love with the Yorkshire landscape. During his work as assistant to veterinarian Donald Sinclair, and later as Sinclair's partner, Wight came to love the Yorkshire people as well. Those people never dreamt that their new, young veterinarian would one day be known and loved worldwide as James Herriot or that their small town would one day become famous as a town named Darrowby.

I, too, was captivated by the Yorkshire countryside. As my train traveled from York to the small town of Thirsk, we passed rolling hills that somehow had a calming effect on me. I was tired from all the traveling I was doing, and it was nice to be lulled by the soothing greens of the hills and dales.

Once leaving the train, however, I was jolted back to reality. No taxi stand. I knew the town was close to two miles away, but in which direction? I spotted a bus stop sign, and as I searched for a bus schedule, an elderly man who'd gotten off the train behind me spoke.

"Did you need help, miss?" he asked. I told him I was going to James Herriot's house but couldn't find the bus schedule.

"Aye." He nodded. "I'm not sure about the bus. It doesn't come very often."

"Well, I suppose I can walk," I said bravely. "Can you tell me in which direction I would head for Thirsk?"

He pointed to our left. "It's that way. I'm going that way if you'd like to come along. Mind you," he warned, "I'm not going all the way to James Herriot's place, but I can drop you off nearby."

I accepted his offer gratefully, but I smiled to myself as I got into his car. I couldn't help remembering my reaction several years before when an Englishwoman had urged me to accept a ride from a stranger.

I'd been on my way to Sissinghurst, the garden made famous by Vita Sackville-West. I was chatting with a woman at the bus stop. (I seem to have lots of interesting encounters at British bus stops.) She mentioned that after I got off the bus, it was a long walk to Sissinghurst—more than a mile. I replied that I enjoyed walking, but she looked skeptical. We chatted about other things, but I could tell it still bothered her.

"Here's an idea," she said finally. "When you leave Sissinghurst, just go out into the parking lot and see if anyone else is leaving. Ask them to drive you down to the village so you won't have that long walk back to the bus stop."

I had tried not to show my shock at this suggestion. I was a woman traveling alone in a foreign country, and she wanted me to accept a ride from a stranger? "Oh—do you really think that would be safe?" I asked.

She had rolled her eyes in exasperation at the silly ideas of some Americans. "These are all going to be gardeners, not serial killers!" I had seen her point, but still, when I left Sissinghurst, I had walked back to the bus stop.

So why was I now quickly accepting a ride from a stranger? True, this man was in his eighties and I could probably outrun him if it came to that, but with his natty suit and courtly manner, I knew it wouldn't come to that. I think it was a combination of trust and becoming more adventurous—plus, I was just plain tired and didn't relish a half-hour walk on narrow British roads.

We chatted on the way to Thirsk, and when I told him I was from Pennsylvania, he was thrilled. "My wife was from Pennsylvania," he said. "She's passed on now, but she was from a small town in western Pennsylvania." He couldn't think of the name, which I could see bothered him.

Shortly after reaching Thirsk, he pulled over and pointed down the street. "This is as far as I can take you, but that's James Herriot's house just up the street." I squinted, wondering how long a walk I had ahead of me. It didn't matter—my driver had been a great help, and I searched in my pocket for some money for petrol. He refused my offer, though, and waved as he pulled away.

I crossed the street, walked a few steps, and then saw the sign for James Herriot's house. I had to smile. My driver had said he "couldn't take me all the way," but the house was less than half a block from where he'd dropped me off.

I opened the red door and entered the world of James Herriot.

James Alfred Wight was born in Sunderland, England, on October 3, 1916. An only child, he moved with his parents to Scotland when he was a baby. As a teenager, he was given a dog as a pet, which began his lifelong love of animals, as well as a lifelong habit of long walks with his dog. Two events coincided with the arrival of his new pet. He read a magazine article that described the veterinary profession, and the director of the

Glasgow Veterinary College gave a talk at his school. After this, Alf Wight was determined to be a vet.

He received a Carnegie bursary to help him pay for his training at Glasgow Veterinary College. Health problems delayed his studies, stretching the usual five-year course into six years, but finally, he graduated and moved back to Sunderland to work as an assistant to a vet. In 1940, he applied for the job of veterinary assistant to Donald Sinclair in Thirsk, a town about fifty miles south of Sunderland. He was hired immediately and, except for serving in the Royal Air Force during World War II, never left.

It was the beginning of World War II, and shortly after Wight arrived in Thirsk, his boss, Donald Sinclair, left for the service. Wight was thrust into the role of sole veterinarian for the practice. On-the-job training never had such a literal meaning. Finding his way around an unfamiliar countryside and dealing with farmers who didn't trust newcomers was a challenge, but Wight wasn't afraid of hard work. He met the challenge and found, to his surprise, that he really enjoyed working with cows. When Sinclair returned from the service, he was thrilled at the increase in profits that his young assistant had achieved.

Alf married Joan Danbury on November 5, 1941, and they lived on the top floor of the veterinary surgery at 23 Kirkgate. After serving in the Royal Air Force, Alf returned home to find that Sinclair had remarried. The Sinclairs wanted the house to themselves, so Alf and Joan found a new place to live for a short while. Sinclair and his new wife soon bought another home, however, and Alf and Joan moved back to 23 Kirkgate. They had two children, a boy, James, and a girl, Rosemary.

Alf's evening conversation usually included sharing funny stories about his work. He'd end these stories with the vow that he'd "write that down someday." Joan finally bought him a typewriter for his birthday, challenging him to stop talking about writing and to do it.

He wrote a few short stories about his days in Glasgow as a veterinary student but had no success in getting them published. He finally decided to follow the standard advice for all beginning writers: Write what you know. He wrote a book about a vet in Yorkshire. Wanting to protect the privacy of his neighbors and clients, he changed the locale of the books to the Yorkshire Dales, about twenty miles from Thirsk. He also set the book in the years before World War II. Otherwise, it followed his own story quite closely: A young vet gets a job in a small town in Yorkshire, has a difficult boss with an irascible brother, and has trouble getting accepted by the local farmers. In the end, he proves himself to the farmers, charms little old ladies, and meets and marries a beautiful local woman.

Although Alf got some encouragement from publishers, they declined to publish the book. It wasn't until a publisher's reader suggested that he write it in the first person that he sat down and seriously revised the book. Alf wrote in the family sitting room, frequently looking up to enjoy something on television and then returning to his writing. Although the practice was thriving now, he still had to do his share of night duty. His writing was frequently interrupted with trips to tend sick farm animals.

Within weeks of sending the revised book to a different publisher, Alf was informed that they would publish it. Now, he had to choose a pseudonym, because at that time, his profession didn't allow advertising, and publishing a book under his own name would be considered advertising. He chose the name James Walsh, but when he checked the veterinary directory, he discovered that there was a vet named James Walsh. He had to come up with another name, and fast. While watching a football game, he noticed a player named Jim Herriot. He liked the way the name sounded, the publisher approved, and from that moment on, Alf Wight became known as James Herriot.

That first book, *If Only They Could Talk*, was published in 1970. Sales were modest in England, as expected for a first book. Wight consoled himself with the thought that at least he'd achieved his goal—he'd gotten published. He'd proven to Joan that it wasn't just talk—he'd done it. He wrote a second book, but he figured that was about it for his writing career.

Then an American publisher, St. Martin's Press, discovered *If Only They Could Talk*. They loved it but thought the book was too short for American tastes. When they heard that Herriot's second book, *It Shouldn't Happen to a Vet*, was about to be published in England, they suggested that the two books be combined for an American edition. Herriot agreed to this, but St. Martin's Press was also concerned that the second book didn't have a definite ending. They asked that it be revised, with the wedding of Helen and James as the finale. Herriot wrote the necessary revisions, and his first two books were published in America under the single title *All Creatures Great and Small*. (His daughter, Rosemary, suggested *Ill Creatures Great and Small*, but the publisher, thankfully, disagreed.)

At the time, St. Martin's Press was in financial trouble, and they were counting on *All Creatures Great and Small* to turn the company around. They began an extensive publicity campaign, sending free copies of the first chapters to bookstores all over the country, and handing out small animal figurines. It didn't take long for reviewers to discover the book and proclaim Herriot's writing as heartwarming, genuine, and hilarious.

Suddenly, James Herriot was a hot property. He was sent on an American tour. A movie adaptation starring Anthony Hopkins was made. In 1978, the BBC called, and Alf Wight's life was changed forever.

Although Wight had changed details and names in his books to protect his privacy and the privacy of his neighbors, fans found Thirsk and James Herriot. Long lines, consisting mostly of Americans, began appearing outside the surgery, winding down the street. Amazed but grateful for the response, Wight gave in to the constant stream of visitors and established Wednesday and Friday afternoons as book-signing days. Although he didn't charge for these signing sessions, he did provide a donation box for an animal charity, and most visitors generously obliged.

Wight enjoyed talking to people but always considered himself a vet, not a writer. He continued his practice at 23 Kirkgate until the early 1990s, when age and declining health forced him to retire. He died on February 23, 1995, of cancer at the age of 78. His son, James, who had become a vet also, continued the practice at 23 Kirkgate until 1996, when the Hambleton District Council bought the building to convert it into a museum.

VISITING THE WORLD OF JAMES HERRIOT

23 Kirkgate
Thirsk, North Yorkshire YO7 1PL
Phone: (0)1845 524234
www.worldofjamesherriot.org
Hours: April 1 to October 31, 10:00 a.m.–5:00 p.m. daily.
      November 1 to March 31, 11:00 a.m.–4:00 p.m. daily.
      Closed December 24–26, and January 1. Closed one
      week in January (dates vary annually).
Admission: adults £6.55, concessions for seniors and families.
    Group rates for 10 or more are available. Groups should
book in advance.
Special evening visits require a minimum of 20 people.
Special activities can be arranged for groups of children.
Booking in advance is essential.
Wheelchair access: lifts to all levels.
Small gift shop.

After paying the entry fee in the small museum shop, go back outside and walk next door to number 23. A brass plaque to the right of the door identifies this as the office of veterinary surgeon Mr. J. A. Wight. On the left, a white wooden box still waits to hold prescriptions for farmers to pick up when the surgery is closed.

Known as Skeldale House in the books, the entrance to The World of James Herriot is small and discreet. The red door doesn't give a hint of the huge complex of rooms hidden behind the modest exterior. The incongruity aptly represents the man who lived and worked there: beneath Alf Wight's modest and retiring exterior was a big heart.

Opening the door is like stepping back sixty years. Visitors enter not only the surgery but also Alf Wight's home, displayed much as it was in the 1940s and 1950s.

In the waiting room on the right (also used as the formal family dining room and, later, as the office), Mrs. Pomfrey waits with her little dog, Tricki Woo, to see their favorite vet. Tricki

Woo barks as visitors enter the room, emphasizing that this was a working veterinary office.

Across the hall, Bing Crosby sings on an old radio in the sitting room. Readers will recognize this room as the one where Herriot nervously awaited his first interview with Siegfried Farnon. Later, this is where Wight and his family would spend the evenings. The books in the cases flanking the fireplace belonged to Wight. The silver tankard on the mantel is a reminder of the surgery's petty cash system.

Down the hall, a small closet filled the role of dispensary. It's kept as it was in the 1940s—full of medicine bottles. In those days, vets were expected to not only diagnose and treat disease but also to mix their own medicines.

Further on, the small breakfast room was the warmest room in the house. The family ate most of their meals here. Between meals, Wight would occasionally do a bit of cat surgery on the dining table.

The family kitchen is next, with the table laid as though a meal is ready to be eaten. The shelves are filled with enough vintage equipment and supplies to make an antique dealer envious.

Exit through the next door, and you're in the garden where the family grew their own vegetables. It was here that James Herriot fell asleep under a tree while waiting for his interview with Siegfried Farnon. The tree is gone, but you can still see the window from which his wife would wave good-bye as he left for work.

A vintage baby-blue Austin Seven seems to be waiting for James Herriot to jump in and head out for a farm call. A sign encourages visitors to take photographs of themselves sitting in the car. This is one of the best things about visiting The World of James Herriot—unlike in most museums, taking photographs is encouraged. The staff is friendly and helpful and dedicated to making sure you get the full experience of Herriot's world.

The Austin's tires are so narrow that one can't help but wonder how Wight ever traveled the bumpy Yorkshire countryside in it. He didn't. Although this car is similar to the model Wight drove in to visit his veterinary clients, it's actually the car that the BBC used in the popular television series *All*

Creatures Great and Small. This is the clue that Wight's life took another direction. Continue back inside the building to discover how Alf Wight became James Herriot.

An informative display relates an enormous amount of information in a small space. From Wight's early days as a veterinary student to his life in Yorkshire, to his success as a writer, it's clear to the visitor that this was a special man. His Olivetti manual typewriter is on display, as is the original manuscript of *It Shouldn't Happen to a Vet.* There's also the rejection letter from the first publisher Wight sent his book to, as well as his first acceptance letter. Copies of his books published in all languages attest to his worldwide popularity.

After a short detour in the fold yard, including a five-minute video summarizing Herriot's life, you step into the next phase of Herriot's career—the BBC studio. Full of lights, cameras, and furniture from the studio set, the dining room and surgery are set up just as they were filmed for the television series. As you progress through the studio, an old-fashioned black plastic phone rings in the surgery. Nobody's around to answer, so you must do it. A panicked voice comes over the line. A horse is ill; Dr. Wight must come at once.

Leave the studio and walk upstairs to the only center in the UK devoted to veterinary science. Old tools are on display with explanations of how they were used, as is information about farm animal diseases and how they were treated. Vets from around the world visit the World of James Herriot to pay homage to the man who inspired them to enter their profession. Herriot's son, James Wight, also a vet, will sometimes give talks to veterinary groups that book in advance.

Another room is full of educational games and exercises to teach children about what it's like to be a vet. Numerous antique veterinary instruments are on display.

Like all well-planned museums, this one exits into the gift shop. The World of James Herriot doesn't have a café, preferring to let visitors patronize the businesses of Thirsk. Continue to wear the museum sticker while walking around town. It will give you a discount in some of the cafés and emphasizes to the locals how much business is brought into the town because of James Herriot.

GETTING THERE

By train: Thirsk is about a 20-minute train ride from York, or about 2 1/2 hours from London's King's Cross Station, with a change in York. At the Thirsk train station, taxi cards are stuck into a board at the station so you can call for a taxi. There is a bus stop near the station, but it has limited times. It's close to a two-mile walk into the town.

By car: From the A1 South: Follow the signs for Masham/Thirsk. This road will take you to the A61 Ripon Road. Right before the traffic lights on the bridge, turn left to Thirsk and follow the signs to Thirsk, approximately eight miles. This brings you to the center of town, known as the Thirsk Market Place.

From the A1 North: Follow the signs for Ripon/Thirsk. Once you leave the motorway, follow the signs to Thirsk on the A61 Ripon Road. Travel approximately eight miles into the cobblestoned center of town, known as the Thirsk Market Place.

Once you have arrived in Thirsk, The World of James Herriot is on Kirkgate on the B1448 to Northallerton. It's best to park in the Market Place and take the three-minute walk to The World of James Herriot. Car parking in the Market Place is restricted to two hours' free disc parking. Parking discs are available from all shops. Alternatively, all-day free parking is available at the Millgate Car Park. From the Market Place, turn onto Kirkgate, following the sign for Northallerton. Just past St. Mary's Church, turn right, which leads to two car parks.

PLACES TO EAT

There are a variety of shops, restaurants, and tearooms in Thirsk. A good restaurant to try is in the Golden Fleece Hotel, phone: (0) 18455 24234. (The Golden Fleece was known as the Drovers Arms in Herriot's books.)

Market days in Thirsk are on Monday and Saturday. There's also a farmer's market in season on the second Monday of each month.

WORKS BY JAMES HERRIOT

If Only They Could Talk—1970

It Shouldn't Happen to a Vet—1971

(In 1970, *All Creatures Great and Small*, published as an American edition,   combined the above two titles, with the wedding of James and Helen added as a new ending.)

Let Sleeping Vets Lie—1973

Vet in Harness—1974

(In 1974, these two titles were combined for an American edition titled *All Things Bright and Beautiful*.)

Vets Might Fly—1976

Vet in a Spin—1977

(In 1977, these two titles were combined for an American edition called *All Things   Wise and Wonderful*.)

James Herriot's Yorkshire—1979

The Lord God Made Them All—1981

Moses the Kitten—1984

James Herriot's Dog Stories—1992

Every Living Thing—1992

RELATED SITES TO VISIT

Church of St Mary Magdalene: (www.stmarysthirsk.org). Farther down Kirkgate from The World of James Herriot is this lovely old church built in 1480. This is where Alf Wight married Joan Danbury in 1941.

The Tourist Information Centre in Thirsk stocks pamphlets outlining a James Herriot Trail. 49 Market Place, Thirsk. Phone: (0)1845 522755

James Herriot's ashes were scattered from the top of **Whitestone Cliffs**, overlooking what he had always declared to be the finest view in England.

ARMCHAIR TRAVELING

www.jamesherriot.org

www.herriotcountry.com

www.thirskfestival.co.uk for information on the Thirsk Festival – an annual event held in early July.

www.herriotdaysout.com to check for Herriot Happenings – events held during Spring Bank Holiday Week

FOR FURTHER READING

The Real James Herriot, A Memoir of My Father by James Wight, 1999

Chapter Five

Bronte Parsonage

Home of the Brontes, 1820–855

Wuthering being a significant provincial adjective, descriptive of the atmospheric tumult to which its station is exposed in stormy weather.

Emily Bronte, *Wuthering Heights*

I may as well admit it up front. I've never been a fan of *Wuthering Heights* or Jane Eyre. All that repressed emotion and angst is just too melodramatic for my taste. And as heroes go, Healthcliff and Mr. Rochester just aren't my type. Heathcliff can be downright nasty, and Mr. Rochester is married, for goodness' sake!

When I made plans to visit the Bronte Parsonage, then, I booked a B&B for just one night. I'd look around, meet with the librarian, and be back in Winchester the next day.

But by the end of the afternoon, I was back in my B&B. "Could I stay an extra night?" I asked the proprietor, a friendly young man who, to my relief, nodded immediately.

It wasn't the Bronte Homestead that had won me over, though. It was the moors. It was raining when I arrived, but that didn't stop me from climbing the hillside behind the parsonage. The rain created the appropriate misty atmosphere for a visit to Bronte country. I looked out over the valley, charmed by the rugged beauty of the landscape. Had it changed at all since the Brontes lived there?

Few authors are associated with a specific landscape as much as Emily Bronte is associated with the windswept moors depicted in *Wuthering Heights*. This harsh landscape was not only an inspiration for Emily's novel but is an obvious metaphor for the isolated, dramatic lives that she and her sisters, Charlotte and Anne, endured.

All of the Bronte sisters were born in a small town called Thornton, but the family moved to Haworth in 1820. Children of a curate, they lived in the parsonage, which was the largest house in Haworth. Living conditions were harsh, however, and disease and death were constant companions to the Brontes. Less than a year and a half after moving to Haworth, their mother, Maria Bronte, died, and Maria's sister, Elizabeth Branwell, moved to Haworth to take care of the family.

The girls' father, Patrick Bronte, knew that when he died, his children would be without a home or legacy. Accordingly, he did his best to educate them so they'd have the means to support themselves. He sent the four eldest girls to a boarding school established especially for the daughters of clergy, but the living conditions were extremely harsh. The only positive aspect of the experience was the later use of the school as the inspiration for Lowood in Charlotte's *Jane Eyre*.

The two youngest Bronte sisters, Maria and Elizabeth, died of tuberculosis. Patrick Bronte brought Charlotte and Emily home and schooled them himself, with Aunt Elizabeth's help.

These early tragedies brought the three sisters and their

brother, Branwell, even closer together. They had always felt like outsiders in Haworth. Their father had been born in Ireland, and his children had the passionate, boisterous nature of their ancestors. This clashed with the reserved Yorkshire people of Haworth, and this clash of temperaments subdued the Bronte children into spending most of their time together. Their father encouraged creative activities, having published four books and some poetry himself. The children spent a good deal of their time writing, drawing, and playing elaborate games, to which only they knew the rules. They created "little books" out of their stories, some of which are now on display in the museum. A gift of a set of toy soldiers for Branwell from his father led to the creation of a land called Angria, where the soldiers had adventures. Later, Emily and Anne created their own land, called Gondal.

As they grew older, the sisters knew they would have to earn a living. Victorian society dictated that teacher or governess was a socially acceptable position for a woman, so these were the professions that the three girls decided to try.

Charlotte and Emily became teachers at a school called Roe Head in 1835, but Emily was so homesick that being away from her beloved moors caused her physical pain. She expressed this longing for the moors in *Wuthering Heights* in Cathy's words "I'm sure I should be myself were I once among the heather on those hills" and in Edgar's words to the dying Cathy: "Now, I wish you were a mile or two up those hills; the air blows so sweetly, I feel that it would cure you."

Emily lasted only three months at Roe Head before escaping back to Haworth. In 1837, she tried another teaching job away from home, but once again, homesickness manifested itself in a physical illness.

The sisters tried working at several places over the next few years. None were completely satisfactory, and they decided the solution was to open their own school. Difficult as it was to leave Haworth once again, Emily forced herself to accompany Charlotte to a school in Belgium to further their studies. They knew this was necessary to become good teachers, and Aunt Elizabeth generously helped finance the plan. Anne took a job as governess at a home near York.

Charlotte blossomed in Brussels, especially with the special tutoring from the owner of the school, Monsieur Heger. Emily, as usual, was miserable being away from home. In 1842, Aunt Elizabeth died, giving Emily the perfect excuse to return home and take over as manager of the parsonage. Charlotte, however, was anxious to return to Belgium after a short visit home, because she'd fallen in love with Monsieur Heger. Unfortunately, he was a married man. Madame Heger suspected Charlotte's strong feelings for her husband, which made the situation tense. Whether Monsieur Heger returned Charlotte's affection is not known, but Charlotte was forced to leave this unbearable situation, and she returned home in 1844.

There, she discovered that a similar affair had developed with her brother, Branwell. Working as a tutor for a young boy in the house where Anne was governess, Branwell had fallen in love with the boy's mother. Forced to leave that position in disgrace, Branwell also returned to Haworth. Addicted to alcohol and drugs, he began a downward spiral of depression and despair.

Anne resigned her position as governess, so by July of 1845, the four siblings were all home again. The sisters advertised for students for their proposed school but got no response. Using part of Aunt Elizabeth's legacy, they decided to self-publish a book called *Poems*. Wanting to protect their privacy, as well as hide the fact that they were women, they published under the names Currer, Ellis, and Acton Bell. The initial of each pseudonym corresponded to the initial of each sister's name. The last name, Bell, may have been taken from the middle name of the curate, Arthur Bell Nicholls, who was assisting Patrick Bronte at the time.

The book was published in May 1846 but sold only two copies. Meantime, Charlotte had completed her first novel, *The Professor*, in 1846, but it was rejected by several publishers.

Undaunted, Charlotte kept writing, and in October 1847, *Jane Eyre* was published. Two months later, Emily's *Wuthering Heights*, and Anne's *Agnes Grey* were also published, although by a different publisher. In June of 1848, Anne's book *The Tenant of Wildfell Hall* was published. All of the books were published under the pseudonyms the girls had chosen for their book of poetry.

The shockingly passionate nature of *Wuthering Heights* upset many readers, and the book didn't sell well. *Agnes Grey* was mostly ignored. *Jane Eyre*, however, was instantly popular, both in England and America, and the identity of Currer Bell was a source of much speculation. In fact, many people, including the publishers, thought the three books were by the same author. Charlotte and Anne were forced to travel to London to prove their identities to Charlotte's publisher, but they swore him to secrecy.

Sadly, along with these glimmerings of success, tragedy struck, not just once, but three times. In September 1848, Branwell died, followed by Emily in December and by Anne in May of 1849. All died of tuberculosis, like their two siblings, although Branwell's death was probably complicated by his addiction to alcohol and opium.

Now Charlotte was left alone with her father. Although she missed her sisters terribly, Charlotte eventually rallied, helped immeasurably by her growing success as an author. She published *Shirley*, the main character of which was based on Emily, and *Villette*, based on her experience with the Hegers. She traveled around the country, including long trips to London, where she met Thackeray and other great thinkers of the day. At first, she kept her identity as the author of *Jane Eyre* secret, but eventually it was revealed, and she enjoyed great celebrity.

Although she now had many friends, Charlotte longed for romance, and she finally found it in her father's assistant, Arthur Bell Nicholls. He'd proposed marriage once, but it had been violently opposed by her father, who feared that Charlotte's delicate constitution would not stand up to the physical rigors of marriage and its inevitable consequences, childbirth. Understandably, Patrick Bronte was also loath to lose his last child. Arthur did not give up, however, and finally, Patrick Bronte relented. Charlotte and Arthur were married on June 29, 1854.

They lived with Charlotte's father at the parsonage, and Arthur took over the curate's duties, as Patrick was becoming old and frail. Soon, Charlotte became pregnant, but the joy of this was marred by a growing illness. On March 31, 1855, Charlotte Bronte died, having lost the baby, and leaving her father and husband alone together. Arthur stayed in the parsonage, as he had promised Charlotte he would do, until Patrick's death in 1861. Then he returned to his native Ireland, where he eventually remarried.

In 1857, Charlotte's first book, *The Professor*, was finally published, but it never reached the popularity of *Jane Eyre*.

The Bronte Society was formed in 1893, and a couple of years later, a small museum was opened in Haworth with some of the Bronte relics on display. In 1927, Sir James Roberts provided funds to build a new rectory, and he bought the parsonage to donate to the Bronte Society. Since then, numerous relics from around the world have been obtained and brought to the parsonage for display. Visiting Haworth enables visitors to learn more about these famous sisters who overcame enormous hardships to become three of the most famous authors in English literature.

VISITING THE BRONTE PARSONAGE

Bronte Parsonage Museum
Church Street, Haworth
Keighley, West Yorkshire BD22 8DR
Phone: (0) 1535 642323
www.bronte.info
Hours: April to September, 10:00 a.m.–5:30 p.m. daily.
      October to March, 11:00 a.m.–5:00 p.m. daily.
      Closed December 24–27 and several weeks in January (exact dates vary annually.)
Admission: adults £6.80, concessions for students, seniors, and families
    Discounts for groups of 10 or more, but must book in advance.
Wheelchair access: to ground floor only.
Large gift shop.

Enter through the front door of the parsonage, paying the entry fee at the small table inside. The docent will recommend the best route to take, determined by how busy the parsonage is at the time.

Mr. Bronte's study is to the right of the entrance hall. It was here that Charlotte told her father that she'd published a book, *Jane Eyre*. He was surprised to hear it but proud of her accomplishment.

Directly across the hall from Mr. Bronte's study is the dining room. The children spent most of their time there, working on their drawing, writing, and painting. In later years, the three sisters would spend the evenings walking continuously around the table, reading aloud from their own work. Emily is said to have died on the sofa in this room.

The next room on the left was probably used as a storeroom in the early days of the family's occupancy of the parsonage. When Charlotte married, however, she had this room remodeled into a study for her husband, Arthur Bell Nicholls. Displays in this room include a wooden board with the Lord's Prayer from the Haworth Church.

The kitchen was refurbished after the Brontes' occupancy of the parsonage. Today, it is furnished as it might have been in the Brontes' time, and some of the family's utensils are on display.

Halfway up the stone stairway stands the long case clock, which Mr. Bronte wound every night on his way to bed. A reproduction of Branwell's portrait of his sisters can also be seen. The original is in the National Portrait Gallery in London.

Upstairs, the tiny servant's room looks out over the cemetery.

The room called Charlotte's room was originally her parents' bedroom. After his wife's death, Patrick Bronte moved across the hall and gave this room to Aunt Elizabeth. After her death, the sisters probably shared the room when they were in residence. Later, Charlotte and her husband occupied this room. Accordingly, relics from all of the Bronte women are to be found in this room, including a sampler made by Mrs. Bronte, a smelling salts bottle belonging to Aunt Elizabeth, letters and drawings by all of the children, and dresses and shoes belonging to Charlotte.

The small room known as the children's study has drawings and paintings on display. Charlotte and Emily were both talented artists, and Emily especially enjoyed drawing nature scenes and animals.

Across the hall is Mr. Bronte's bedroom, with reproduction furniture recreating the way the bedroom probably looked during his time. Branwell died in this room. Branwell's studio shows the type of work he did during his short career as a portrait painter. Beyond the studio is a wing added on after the Bronte's time,

Downstairs is the Bonnell Room, named after an American who donated his collection of Bronteana to the museum. Various items of the museum's vast collection are on rotating display here but usually include copies of the little books that the children created, as well as Charlotte's and Emily's writing desks, plus letters and personal items. The massive apostle's cupboard, described in *Jane Eyre*, is a feature of the room.

Although the museum does a beautiful job of presenting the life of the Brontes, a complete understanding of their life requires a ramble on the moors. The Tourist Information Centre presents several options outlining walks in the countryside surrounding Haworth, from a single pamphlet showing a few paths, to booklets describing detailed walks.

The moors are actually more isolated now than they were in the Brontes' day. Then, stone quarries offered the main employment for local residents and numerous farmhouses dotted the landscape. Most of the quarries are abandoned now, and the farmhouses are gone or dilapidated. This really just adds to the lonely, picturesque quality of the countryside.

Much speculation has surrounded the inspiration for the home in *Wuthering Heights*. Most people seem to agree that Emily probably based the house itself on a house in the area called High Sunderland Hall, which has since been demolished. The site of Wuthering Heights, however, was probably the farm known as Top Withins. The surrounding landscape of the farm seems to match the overall feeling of Wuthering Heights. A house called Ponden Hall seems to have been the inspiration for the Linton's home, Thrushcross Grange.

Don't miss the sculpture on top of the hill known as the Literary Landscape. In the 1990s, a sculptor was commissioned to create a piece of art to represent the literary associations of the moors. He sculpted a set of cement books that look as though they're growing out of the ground.

GETTING THERE

By train: Take the train from London's King's Cross Station to Leeds, then transfer to a train to Keighley. From there, it's about three miles to Haworth. You can take a taxi from the Keighley train station (but will usually have to call for one) or walk into Keighley and take a bus—664, 665, or 720—asking the driver to let you off close to the Bronte Parsonage. Or, for a more leisurely and scenic route, from the Keighley train station, take the Keighley and Worth Valley Steam Railway. This runs daily in the summer but only on weekends and for special events during the remainder of the year. It has limited departure times.

PLACES TO EAT:

The Black Bull: Serving the usual pub food, this inn makes the most of the fact that Branwell Bronte did a lot of drinking here.

The Old White Lion: Serving good food, this establishment is divided into two sections: one section a pub, the other a more formal dining room. Patrick Bronte attended political meetings here.

WORKS BY THE BRONTES

By all three:
Poems—1846
By Charlotte Bronte:
Jane Eyre—1847
Shirley—1849
Villette—1853
The Professor—1857
By Emily Bronte:
Wuthering Heights—1847
By Anne Bronte:

Agnes Grey—1847
The Tenant of Wildfell Hall—1848

RELATED SITES TO VISIT

St. Michael and All Angels Church, Haworth, West Yorkshire: Burial place of Emily and Charlotte Bronte. Although the majority of the church was demolished and rebuilt in 1879, a stone plaque memorializes the final resting place of Emily, Charlotte, and Branwell, as well as of their mother and father and two younger sisters, Maria and Elizabeth.

St. Mary's Churchyard, Scarborough, North Yorkshire: Burial place of Anne Bronte. **Wycoller**: The village of Wycoller was the inspiration for *Jane Eyre*. Ferndean Manor was based on Wycoller Hall.

National Portrait Gallery, London (www.npg.org.uk): The gallery contains a painting of Anne, Charlotte, and Emily by Branwell, with Branwell painted out. The museum also contains a portrait of Charlotte painted by George Richmond. Emily is depicted in a fragment of a picture which is thought to have originally included Anne, Charlotte, Emily, and Branwell. The nearest Underground stop is Charing Cross on the Northern and Bakerloo lines, or Leicester Square on the Piccadilly line.

British Library, London (www.bl.uk): This has Bronte memorabilia, including the original manuscript of *Jane Eyre*. The nearest Underground stop is King's Cross/St. Pancras on the Northern, Piccadilly, Victoria, Circle, Metropolitan, and Hammersmith & City lines.

Westminster Abbey, London (www.westminster-abbey.org): A memorial stone to the Brontes is in Poet's Corner. The nearest Underground stop is Westminster on the Circle, District, and Jubilee lines.

ARMCHAIR TRAVELING

www.bronte.info for information about the Bronte Society – founded on December 16, 1893. Phone: (0) 1535 640195 www.visithaworth.com for more information about visiting Bronte country, including guided walks.

FOR FURTHER READING

Dark Quartet by Lynn Reid Banks, 1977

Path to the Silent Country by Lynn Reid Banks, 1979

The Life of Charlotte Bronte by Elizabeth Gaskell, 1857; reprinted by the Oxford University Press, 1996

Emily Bronte, A Chainless Soul by Katherine Frank, 1990

Chapter Six

D. H. LAWRENCE
BIRTHPLACE MUSEUM

Home of D. H. Lawrence, 1885–1887

[T]he cottages of these coal-miners, in blocks and pairs here and there, together with odd farms and homes of the stockingers, straying over the parish, formed the village of Bestwood.

D. H. Lawrence, *Sons and Lovers*

*D*avid Herbert Richards Lawrence was born on September 11, 1885, in the coal-mining town of Eastwood, Nottinghamshire. His father was a coal miner, and David Lawrence—called Bert—was expected to be a coal miner. Instead, he became a writer, and his early work drew heavily on his childhood experience of growing up in a coal-mining town.

Although he called his hometown the "country of my heart," he also hated it and what it had done to his family, especially his mother. As an adult, he traveled around the world, searching, perhaps, for a better life, but his writing and painting were so controversial that he struggled to achieve public approval of his work. Although he escaped the life of a coal miner, he never really escaped the poverty of his youth.

Lawrence did fairly well at school, earning a scholarship to send him to high school. He worked in a factory for a short time, but the first of many illnesses forced him to give that up. He then worked as a teacher and went on to University College in Nottingham in 1908.

In 1907, he won a short story contest in the *Nottingham Guardian*, and in 1909, he had poems published in *The English Review*. His first book, *The White Peacock*, was published in 1911.

Lawrence's mother, a former teacher, was a major influence on his life. Lawrence wrote of this relationship, and of his mother's hatred of his father, in his novel *Sons and Lovers*, published in 1913. Like Paul Morel, the protagonist of *Sons and Lovers*, Lawrence helped his mother die when she became ill, even though he was overcome with grief at the loss.

In 1912, Lawrence met Frieda von Richthofen Weekley, who was married to one of his former professors. She left her husband and children and ran off with Lawrence to Bavaria, where Lawrence was arrested on suspicion of being a British spy. This type of suspicion was repeated when the couple, having married in 1914, returned to England. They were accused of being German spies and were forced to leave their home in Cornwall.

They left England in 1919, beginning a voluntary exile that Lawrence called his savage pilgrimage. They traveled extensively through Europe and America. Wherever they traveled, Lawrence wrote about that place; Italy, America, and Mexico all received the Lawrence treatment, either in travelogues, novels, or nonfictions. His book about classical American literature was well-received, but other works were not.

Lawrence had begun painting in the 1920s and in 1929 had an exhibition of his work in London. It was judged too controversial because of its violence and blatant sexuality. Thirteen paintings were confiscated by police. To save the paintings from being destroyed, Lawrence was forced to agree to remove them from England and to never exhibit in England again.

The Lawrences finally settled in Taos, New Mexico, where he bought a 160-acre ranch in exchange for the manuscript of *Sons and Lovers*. The D. H. Lawrence Ranch, as it is now known, was originally owned by Mabel Dodge Luhan, an art patroness who encouraged Lawrence's interest in art.

Lawrence was plagued by frail health throughout his life, and on March 2, 1930, he succumbed to tuberculosis while visiting France. Frieda had him cremated. Later, she had his ashes brought to the ranch in Taos, where she was, by then, living with her third husband, Angelo Ravagli.

Frieda left Ravagli nine of Lawrence's confiscated paintings, and after her death, Ravagli sold them to the owner of the La Fonda Hotel in Taos, where they are on exhibit today.

VISITING THE D. H. LAWRENCE BIRTHPLACE

8a Victoria Street
Eastwood, Nottingham
Phone: (0)1773 717353
www.dhlawrenceheritage.org
Hours: April to October, 10:00 a.m.–7:00 p.m.
   November to March, 10:00 a.m.–6:00 p.m.
   Closed Mondays and Saturdays
   Closed Christmas week

Admission: free weekdays
 Weekends and Bank Holidays: Adults £2.00, concessions to children and families.
 Joint tickets available with the Durban House Heritage Centre
 Free admission every day to Broxtowe Borough Council residents

Wheelchair access: entire centre
Small gift shop

The D. H. Lawrence Birthplace Museum is located in Eastwood, near Nottingham. It is one of four houses the family occupied in Eastwood. It's owned by the D. H. Lawrence Heritage and is managed by Broxtowe Borough Council.

You'll enter the museum through the house next door, going through the museum shop. There are only a few original items on display from the Lawrence family, but the house is nicely furnished with period furniture and accessories.

Visitors are given a guided tour of the house, which takes approximately 45 minutes. The guide will explain the significance of each room (parlor, kitchen, yard, washroom, parents' bedroom, children's bedroom, attic).

There is a small exhibition of Lawrence's early original watercolor paintings. Photocopies of his later paintings are displayed on a panel. The latest addition to the collection has been Lawrence's gravestone, which was commissioned by Frieda. She kept it with her in New Mexico, but it's been on display here since September 11, 2009, the anniversary of his birthday.

You'll finish your tour with a 10-minute DVD on D. H. Lawrence's life.

GETTING THERE

By train: Langley Mill train station is about two miles away.

By bus: Trent Barton buses on both the Rainbow Line Number 1 Riley/Nottingham and the Black Cat bus Mansfield/Derby. The bus stop is located a short walk away, less than five minutes' walk. Bus service information: (www.nctx.co.uk)

By car: From the M1 Junction 26, take the A610 toward Eastwood and follow the brown "D. H. Lawrence Heritage" tourism signs.

From M1 Junction 27, take the A608 through Brinsley toward Eastwood.

As you get into Eastwood, there are two sets of brown heritage signs. They will take you to either the museum or to Durban House Heritage Centre. Please note that only Durban

House has its own car park, but the two sites are only about five minutes apart by foot.

D. H. Lawrence Heritage is situated close to IKEA Retail Park, which is also signposted from the motorway.

PLACES TO EAT

Hatters Tea Shop: next to the Durban Heritage Centre. This lovely tea shop features breakfast, lunch, and afternoon teas. The name is taken from a line in *Lady Chatterley's Lover*: "And the authorities felt ridiculous, and behaved in a rather ridiculous fashion, and it was all a mad-hatter's tea party for a while." Open Tuesday to Fridays and Sundays, 10:00 a.m. – 4:00 p.m.

WORKS BY D. H. LAWRENCE

The White Peacock—1911
The Trespasser—1912
Sons and Lovers—1913
The Prussian Officer and Other Stories—1914
The Rainbow—1915
Look! We Have Come Through—1917
The Lost Girl—1920
Women in Love—1920
England, My England—1921
Fantasia of the Unconscious—1922
Aaron's Rod—1922
Birds, Beasts and Flowers (poetry)—1923
Kangaroo—1923
The Plumed Serpent—1926
Lady Chatterley's Lover—1928
The Man Who Died—1929

RELATED SITES

Durban House Heritage Centre, Durban: This house is five minutes' walk from the Birthplace Museum. It features a temporary exhibition space called the Rainbow Gallery, plus displays on mining and on Lawrence.

D. H. Lawrence Heritage
Mansfield Road
Eastwood, Nottingham
NG16 3DZ
Phone: (0) 1773 717353

The Blue Line Trail: Modeled on the Red Line Freedom Trail in Boston, MA, USA, the Blue Line Trail takes you past the four Eastwood houses in which Lawrence lived and other related sites. A copy of the trail can be found at the Broxtowe Council web site (www.broxtowe.gov.uk) by searching for Lawrence.

Taos, New Mexico, USA (www.lafondataos.com): The largest collection of Lawrence's paintings is now at La Fonda Hotel in Taos, New Mexico. Several, including *Boccaccio Story* and *Resurrection*, are at the Humanities Research Center of the University of Texas at Austin.

ARMCHAIR TRAVELING

www.dh-lawrence.org.uk University of Nottingham has a collection of Lawrence manuscripts and other research materials available.

www.broxtowe.co.uk for information on the D. H. Lawrence Festival.

www.nottinghamcity.gov.uk for things to do in Nottingham. Search for the **Museum of Nottingham Life** for information about what life was like in Lawrence's time. The museum also has a plastic cast of Lawrence's signature.

www.dhlsna.com is the web site of the D. H. Lawrence Society in North America. Part of their mission is to preserve Lawrence's ranch in Taos, New Mexico.

FURTHER READING

D. H. Lawrence: The Life of an Outsider by John Worthen, 2005

The Selected Letters of D. H. Lawrence, edited by James T. Boulton, 1997

Chapter Seven

The Charles Dickens Museum

Home of Charles Dickens, 1837–1839

The sky was dark and gloomy, the air was damp and raw, the streets were wet and sloppy. The smoke hung sluggishly above the chimney-tops as if it lacked the courage to rise, and the rain came slowly and doggedly down, as if it had not even the spirit to pour.

Charles Dickens, *The Pickwick Papers*

Many people associate Dickens with his novels of Victorian London, which exposed the plight of poor people and abused children of England, but less known, perhaps, is that Dickens also championed the cause of international copyright laws and was one of the first, and amazingly successful, authors to do literary readings of their work.

Dickens was born on February 7, 1812, in the town of Portsmouth. He was the second of eight children. In 1815, the family moved to London. In 1824, his father, John Dickens, was imprisoned at Marshalsea Debtors' Prison, in Southwark, on the southern side of the Thames River. Charles got work at Warren's Blacking Factory, which made what would today be called shoe polish. The factory was located where Charing Cross Station now sits. Dickens hated his work but remembered it later, using the experience in *Little Dorrit* and *David Copperfield*. While working at the blacking factory, he worked with a man named Bob Fagin. Although Dickens used this man's name for the villain in *Oliver Twist*, the fictional character was quite different from his real-life inspiration. Fagin taught Charles how to do his work more efficiently, and the two became friends.

Dickens was hardworking and ambitious, but he didn't find much support at home. His parents put what little money they had into educating their daughter Fanny, and Dickens had to work for a living instead of furthering his own education. This didn't seem to make him bitter toward his sister, however, as he used her as the basis for Fan, Scrooge's beloved sister in *A Christmas Carol*.

In 1827, Dickens found work in a solicitor's office called Ellis and Blackmore. He thought of going into law himself but found he hated working in the office. His low opinion of lawyers, depicted in *Pickwick Papers* and *Great Expectations*, seems to have been formed at this time.

He learned shorthand and in 1829 got a job as a court stenographer for the *Morning Chronicle*, reporting on Parliament. His first fictional story, "A Dinner at Poplar Walk," was published in 1833 in *Monthly Magazine*. Several more stories followed, although he had to eventually decline to write more, as he wasn't paid for them. Around the same time, the editor of the *Morning Chronicle* decided to publish an evening edition and asked Dickens to write some stories for it. This time, Dickens would be paid for his work, over and above his wages as a reporter.

Dickens loved to walk the streets of London, especially at night and in the early morning. He used this time to observe the different classes of people in different areas of the city. He especially noticed the differences in their speech and their way of life. His articles for the *Chronicle* described the people and places he saw during these long walks, from the colorful fruit sellers in Covent Garden to the slums of Seven Dials, to the development of the wealthy Eaton Square. He signed his articles under the pen name Boz, which was the nickname of one of his younger brothers. In 1836, these scenes of London life were collected into his first book, *Sketches by Boz*.

Dickens also toyed with the notion of acting, but was sick on the day of his planned audition and gave up on that idea.

In 1830, he met and fell in love with Maria Beadnell, but her family didn't approve of him, and the romance ended. He didn't forget Maria, however. He used her as the basis of the character Dora in *David Copperfield*, which was his favorite of his own books.

In 1834, he met Catherine Hogarth, whose father was the music critic for the *Morning Chronicle*. Charles and Catherine married on April 2, 1836.

The Pickwick Papers was published in monthly installments and proved to be a rousing success. Dickens was now able to support himself and his family with his novels. They moved into the house on Doughty Street, now the Dickens House Museum, and Catherine's sister, Mary, moved in with them. Dickens was very close to Mary; some say he was in love with her. He was devastated when she died in 1937, and wore a ring of hers for the rest of his life.

Over the next twenty years, Dickens continued to write novels in monthly installments. Much of his work was set in London, but his work became so popular that people waited breathlessly for the next installment of all of his works. The first recorded traffic jam in New York City was in 1840 when the ship came in with the last three installments of *The Old Curiosity Shop*. Hundreds of people waited at the pier to hear if Little Nell was dead.

Dickens also edited and wrote for two weekly magazines— first *Household Words*, then *All the Year Round*, which he continued working on until his death.

Dickens traveled extensively. Several times, he visited Italy, and he also sailed to America, writing about the people he met and the things he saw. Although he enjoyed traveling, he was on a mission. He was unhappy about copyright laws that allowed American publishers to print his books without paying him any royalties. He was sure that he could persuade Americans to his case, but he was disillusioned with their condescending response to his criticisms. Americans, for their part, were equally stunned at Dickens's hostility. They had welcomed him with open arms, and here he was, attacking them. Dickens didn't back down. He continued to fight copyright laws both in lawsuits and in his writing. His book *American Notes* was published in 1842. Its scathing depiction of Americans infuriated them even more. Still, the copyright laws in America didn't change until well after Dickens's death, when American writers finally found the shoe on the other foot: Canadian publishers were printing American books without paying royalties.

In addition to his rigorous writing and editing duties, Dickens was finally able to realize his early acting ambitions. He started an amateur theatrical company in London, writing and then performing in some of these works.

He also channeled his acting abilities into readings he gave to the public, dramatically portraying each of the characters in his works. Although he had begun doing this for charity—like Thackeray and Carlyle before him—he quickly began to resent the time and energy the readings took. He started charging for them, which began a whole new career. He thoroughly enjoyed the contact with and the response from his audiences.

In 1856, Dickens fulfilled a childhood dream by purchasing a home in Kent called Gad's Hill Place. He had fallen in love with this house when he and his father had passed it during a walk when Dickens was a child. His father had told him that if he worked hard he could someday own a house like that. Dickens was thrilled to see this dream come true.

By 1858, Dickens and his wife, who had borne him 10 children, were separated, although they never officially divorced. Around the time of his separation, Dickens and his great friend Wilkie Collins wrote a play together called *The Frozen Deep.*

An actress named Ellen Ternan was in the play, and Dickens fell in love with her. They began an affair that lasted the rest of his life.

Dickens worked almost frantically now, filling his days with writing, editing, and lecturing. He worked until he became sick, and he continued working even then. Dickens died of a stroke on June 9, 1870. His last unfinished manuscript, *The Mystery of Edwin Drood*, was published after his death.

VISITING THE CHARLES DICKENS MUSEUM

48 Doughty Street
London WC1N 2LX
Phone: (0)20740 52127
www.dickensmuseum.com
Hours: daily 10:00 a.m.–5:00 p.m.
Admission: Adults £7.00
Concessions to seniors, children, and families
Group discounts to 10 or more; book in advance
Small gift shop.

Dickens and his wife moved into this house in 1837, shortly after the birth of their first son. The house had been built in the early 19th century. At that time, Doughty Street had gates and gatekeepers at each end of the street to maintain privacy of the residents.

The Charles Dickens Museum is owned by the London County Council, under the guidance of the Board of Trustees for the Charles Dickens Museum. The museum was established in 1925.

Pay your entry fee at the small shop at the back of the ground floor, and if the weather is fine, step outside into the tiny garden. The step leading into the garden was removed from the front of St. George's Church in Southwark. It is on this step that the heroine and her husband pause at the end of *Little Dorrit*.

Next, begin a tour of the house in the basement with a short film that summarizes Dickens's life. On display in the basement is the desk Dickens used when he worked at the solicitors office from May 1827 to November 1828. Also on display is a grille from the Marshallsea Prison, where Dickens's father was imprisoned for bad debts. This basement was used by the servants in the 19th century. The library, which now contains hundreds of books by Dickens, in many languages, was used as a kitchen in his time.

Proceed upstairs to the second floor and work your way back down. Take note on the stairway of a number of memorabilia items, including the Golden Arm, which figured in *A Tale of Two Cities*.

On the second floor, at the back of the house, is the bedroom in which Dickens's sister-in-law, Mary Hogarth, died. This room also has photos and memorabilia relating to Dickens's acting career.

The front room was originally his bedroom, shared with his wife, Catherine. It now contains interesting articles and photographs about the readings Dickens did in Europe and America. His readings were so popular (up to 4,000 people in an audience) that, by the time he reached New York, ticket sales were limited to four per person, to discourage ticket scalpers. When that wasn't enough, the requirement was added that every ticket buyer had to be wearing a hat! A photograph of ticket-buyers wearing hats is on display here.

Next to this room is the Dressing Room, which displays the reading desk that Dickens had specially designed for his readings. It was made in 1859, and he took it on every performance with him, even to America.

On the first floor is the room Dickens used as a study. He was rather superstitious and liked to have certain objects on his desk while he wrote. His mascot was a monkey, and on his desk, one could usually find a china monkey and a brass one.

Aspiring writers can learn much from Dickens's writing habits. He was very organized and advocated writing what you know. He also understood the importance of discipline. The only time he missed a deadline was when Mary Hogarth died.

Also on display are two beloved pictures. One, *The Empty Chair* by Sir Samuel Luke Fildes, was sketched after Dickens's death, and depicts his empty chair and desk at his home, Gad's Hill. The other picture, *Dickens's Dream*, painted by Robert Buss but based partly on *The Empty Chair*, depicts a sleeping Dickens surrounded by images of his fictional characters.

The original handwritten manuscripts from *Pickwick Papers* and *Nicholas Nickleby* are also on display in the study. Once he became popular, Dickens began preserving his manuscripts. Others are on display at the Victoria and Albert Museum in London.

In this room, you can also learn about the special paper that Dickens used for his stories. The novels were written in 20 monthly installments, and he was strictly limited to a certain number of words per story. He knew the value of ending each chapter with a cliffhanger. It meant his readers would build up a frenzy of anticipation for the next installment. He used this special paper because it made it easy for him to see how far he had to go in the installment.

The dining room is on the ground floor and is rather interesting architecturally, as the back wall and two doors are curved. Some of the Dickens family china and silver is on display here, as is the massive mahogany sideboard that was originally used at Gad's Hill.

Those interested in the Dickens family tree should stop in the morning room, which has this rather massive document on display.

In the hallway on the ground floor is a clock from Gad's Hill. Take a moment to read the letter that Dickens wrote concerning the repair of the clock. It reveals his delightful sense of humor. Also in the hallway is a window from his boyhood home in Bayham Street, Camden Town. This window is described in the burglary scene of *Oliver Twist*.

Allow about 1 ½ hours to thoroughly examine the exhibits. There are more than 10,000 items in the museum collection, so the displays are changed periodically. This means that visiting more than once is likely to turn up new items of interest.

GETTING THERE

Nearest Underground station: Russell Square on the Piccadilly line. About ten minutes' walk. On exiting the Russell Square station, turn right on Bernard Street, then right onto Grenville. Take the next left onto Guilford Street and then right onto Doughty Street. The Charles Dickens Museum is on the left, with a blue plaque on the building, and a green sign outside. Ring for entry.

PLACES TO EAT

The new Museum Café is open daily from 10:00 a.m. to 5:00 p.m.

WORKS BY DICKENS

Dates refer to the year the full volume was published.
Sketches by Boz—1836
The Posthumous Papers of the Pickwick Club—1837
Oliver Twist—1838
Sketches of Young Gentlemen—1838
Memoirs of Joseph Grimaldi (originally published under the pen name Boz)—1938
Nicholas Nickleby—1839
The Old Curiosity Shop—1840
Barnaby Rudge—1841
American Notes—1842
Martin Chuzzlewitt—1843
A Christmas Carol—1843
The Chimes—1844
The Cricket on the Hearth—1845
Dombey and Son—1846
David Copperfield—1850
Bleak House—1852
Hard Times—1854
Little Dorrit—1857
A Tale of Two Cities—1859
Great Expectations—1861
Our Mutual Friend—1864
Edwin Drood (uncompleted)—1870

RELATED SITES

Westminster Abbey, London (www.westminster-abbey.org): Dickens is buried here. The nearest Underground station is at Westminster on the Circle and District lines.

Victoria & Albert Museum, London (www.vam.ac.uk): Original Dickens manuscripts are part of the Forster Collection. The nearest Underground station is South Kensington on the Piccadilly, Circle, and District lines.

National Portrait Gallery, London (www.npg.org.uk): The NPG has 80 paintings of Dickens in its collection, but there's usually only one on display. This painting of Dickens by his close friend Daniel Maclise was also used for the frontispiece of *Nicholas Nickleby*. The nearest Underground station is Charing Cross on the Northern and Bakerloo lines, or Leicester Square on the Piccadilly line.

The British Museum, London (www.britishmuseum.org): Dickens got his reader's ticket at the British Library on his 18th birthday. Originally housed in the British Museum, the British Library is now located near King's Cross Station, but the Reading Room at the British Museum still commemorates Dickens's use of the library on their list of famous readers right inside the entry to the Reading Room. The nearest Underground station is Holborn or Russell Square on the Piccadilly line.

British Library, London (www.bl.uk): The British Library has manuscript pages from chapter 15 of *Nicholas Nickleby*. The nearest Underground station is King's Cross Station on the Victoria, Northern, Hammersmith & City, Circle, and Metropolitan lines.

Charles Dickens Birthplace
393 Old Commercial Road
Portsmouth
Phone: (0)2392 827261
www.charlesdickensbirthplace.co.uk
Hours: May to September, 10:00 a.m.–5:30 p.m.
Closed October to April, except for Dickens's birthday, February 7
Admission: Adults £3.50; concessions for seniors, children, and families.
Group discounts if booked in advance

The Dickens birthplace has three rooms open to the public: the parlor, the dining room, and the bedroom where Dickens was born. None of the original furnishings are there, but the rooms are furnished in the appropriate style of the day. There are a few bits of memorabilia, including the couch on which Dickens died at Gad's Hill Place. The house is small and has narrow stairs and so is not wheelchair accessible.

GETTING THERE

By train: The Portsmouth and Southsea Rail Station is about 3/4 of a mile away.

By car: M27 Junction 12 is 2 1/2 miles away.

ARMCHAIR TRAVELING

www.dickensfellowship.org The Dickens Fellowship was founded in 1902. It's based at the Dickens House Museum in London. This web site is based in England but has links and information about chapters around the world.

www.victorianweb.org/authors/dickens This web site is all about Victorian writers.

www.americanfriendsofdickens.com is a group of American fans of Dickens who support the Charles Dickens House.

FOR FURTHER READING

Oxford Reader's Companion to Charles Dickens by Paul Schlicke, 2000

Charles Dickens: His Tragedy and Triumph by Edgar Johnson, 1952, revised 1977

The Life of Charles Dickens by Forster, 1872–1874

Chapter Eight

KEATS HOUSE

Home of John Keats, 1818–1820

That thou, light-winged Dryad of the trees,
In some melodious plot
Of beechen green, and shadows numberless,
Singest of summer in full-throated ease.

John Keats, "Ode to a Nightingale"

*I*n the summer of 1819, a nightingale nested in a plum tree outside the home of John Keats in Hampstead Heath, near London. Keats spent several hours sitting under the plum tree, listening to the nightingale sing. The beauty of the bird's song inspired him to write the poem that is now known as "Ode to a Nightingale." Still in mourning for his brother, who had recently died from tuberculosis, Keats wrote a poem celebrating the beauty of the bird's song tempered with the knowledge that the bird would one day die. Keats suggests that people will always be able to enjoy another nightingale's song because nature is always renewing itself. This theme of the beauty of life, as well as the pain of illness and death, is one that Keats used extensively in his work.

Visiting Keats House and contemplating the plum tree that now replaces the one Keats sat under, one feels a strong empathy for this Romantic poet who died at age 25. The sadness of his early death, and his passionate love for the girl next door, permeate every room of Keats House, yet, like those who hear a nightingale sing, people will always be able to enjoy Keats's poetry.

John Keats's father, Thomas Keats, worked for an inn and livery stable in London. In 1794, Thomas married the boss's daughter, Frances Jennings. John, their first son, was born on October 31, 1795. Two more sons and a daughter soon followed. When Frances's father retired, Thomas Keats took over the business. By now he could afford to send John to an excellent school. John was a dedicated student, absorbing everything the school had to offer. He also became friends with the headmaster's son, Charles Cowden Clarke, and this was a friendship that would last the rest of his life.

John's happy childhood was soon marred by tragedy. His father died in a fall from a horse in 1804. His mother quickly remarried, but the marriage was short-lived. In 1805, his grandfather Jennings died. These events not only were emotionally wrenching for the children but also caused a variety of legal and financial hassles that would plague them for years. The children were sent to live with their grandmother, and for a while, John's mother disappeared. She returned in 1809. John immersed himself in his schoolwork, but soon, more tragedy would hit the family. His mother contracted tuberculosis (then known as consumption) and died in 1810.

John knew he had to support his brothers and sister, so he quit school to become an apothecary's apprentice. He didn't give up his love of literature, however. He read whenever he could and had long discussions about literature with his school friend, Charles Clarke. He began writing poetry and started asking Clarke's advice on it. Clarke was encouraging. In 1816, John's first published poem, "O Solitude," appeared in the *Examiner*. John met with the editor of the *Examiner*, Leigh Hunt, who was impressed with the poems Keats showed him. Shortly afterward, Keats passed the apothecary exam but then made the decision that would change his life. He would be a poet rather than an apothecary.

The next few years were full of hard work, triumphs, and more tragedy. In 1817, Keats's first book, *Poems*, was published. This, as well as much of his later work, was lavishly praised by some and viciously condemned by others.

In 1818, his book *Endymion*, inspired by Greek mythology, was published, mostly to hostile criticism. *Blackwood's* magazine attacked Keats as a member of the Cockney School of Poetry, an insult referring not just to somebody born in London but also to a vulgar person. Critics didn't respect his work because he didn't have a classical or university education. In the preface of the book, however, Keats himself admits that the book is flawed and immature, so he apparently wasn't too concerned about criticism.

Keats and his friend Charles Brown spent the summer of 1818 walking through the Lake District of England, as well as through Scotland and Northern Ireland. They planned to visit William Wordsworth along the way, but Wordsworth wasn't home, so the two poets never did meet. This trip, however, with its long rambles through the gorgeous countryside of the Lake District, served to solidify Keats's identification with nature.

On his return home, Keats was dealt another devastating blow. His brother Tom was ill with tuberculosis and, in December, Tom died.

Keats moved into Brown's house, then known as Wentworth Place, near Hampstead Heath. Thus began the year of Keats's most prolific work. He wrote his major odes, including "Ode to Autumn" and "Ode on a Grecian Urn," as well as one of his finest poems, "La Belle Dame sans Merci."

One source of his inspiration may have been the girl next door, Fanny Brawne, who, with her mother and brother, lived in the other half of the house. A romance began between the two, and Keats became engaged to Brawne. His love letters to Fanny Brawne are considered to be some of the most passionate love letters ever written.

Tragedy struck once again, however. By early 1820, Keats became ill with what was eventually diagnosed as tuberculosis. At the time, one-third of London's population died of tuberculosis. Having watched his mother and brother die of the same disease, Keats knew what was ahead of him.

Keats was advised by his doctor to seek warmer weather, and, in September of 1820, he and his friend Joseph Severn set sail for Italy. Unfortunately, the attempted cure may have hastened his death, as the journey took four weeks, followed by 10 days of quarantine on the boat upon its arrival in Italy.

Keats died in Rome on February 23, 1821. He's buried there, with a tombstone, which, at his request, doesn't mention his name, only the sentiment: "Here lies one whose name was writ in water." Joseph Severn's tombstone, next to Keats's, refers to Severn as a friend of Keats. The house where Keats died is open to the public and bears a plaque commemorating him.

VISITING KEATS HOUSE
The City of London Corporation administers Keats House.
Keats Grove
Hampstead, London NW3 2RR
Phone: (0) 207332 3868
www.keatshouse.cityoflondon.gov.uk
Hours: From Easter (exact date varies annually) to October
 31, Tuesday to Sunday:
 All visitors: 1:00 p.m.–5:00 p.m.
 Schools and pre-booked group visits only: Tuesday to
 Friday 10:00 a.m.–12:00 p.m.
 From November 1 to Easter:
 All visitors, Friday to Sunday, 1:00 p.m.–5:00 p.m.
 Schools and pre-booked groups: Tuesday to Thursday
 10:00 p.m.–5:00 p.m. (must pre-book)
 Closed on all Mondays except bank holidays.
Special events such as poetry readings are scheduled throughout the year. Call for details.

Admission: Adults £5.00, concessions to seniors and adults
Ticket good for one year
Garden: free daily
Small gift shop.

Bustling, trendy Hampstead is now part of London, but in Keats's day, it was considered country. The house itself, divided into two homes when Keats lived there, was converted into one home about twenty years after his death. It opened as a museum in 1925, and today visitors can tour all of the rooms.

The garden in front of the house features the famous plum tree, although it's not the original. Other borders in the garden reflect Keats's poetry themes of Melancholy and Autumn. Several benches scattered around the garden encourage visitors to linger and relax. The surrounding brick walls help to mask the noise of people enjoying Hampstead Heath.

After paying the entry fee, visitors proceed into a museum room, which features various busts of Keats and friends as well as paintings and other memorabilia. The first two rooms are known as the Brawne rooms, as these are on the Brawne family's side of the house.

Brown's sitting room, the first room on the left, was probably used for entertaining. The windows give a lovely view of the garden. When Keats fell ill, he was moved to this room so he could look out onto Hampstead Heath. It was while walking on the heath in 1819 that he met Samuel Coleridge for the first time. During another walk on the heath, Keats was inspired to write the poem "I Stood Tiptoe Upon a Little Hill." Today, the view of the heath is blocked by other houses and by the brick walls that act as a boundary to the property, but Keats would have had a clear view of this parkland and the grazing sheep.

Across the hall, Keats's sitting room gives the best feel for his presence in this house. On display are his books, inkstand, and writing desk. In front of the fireplace, two chairs, set at an angle to one another, seem out of place at first, but the portrait above the fireplace solves the puzzle. The painting is of Keats by his friend Joseph Severn and is titled *Keats Reading*. It depicts the same two chairs in the same room. Keats is sitting in one chair, his arm resting on the back of the other. The original of this painting hangs in the National Portrait Gallery in London.

In the back of the house is a sunroom, added on after Keats's time. Poetry readings and other special events frequently take place here.

Upstairs is Keats's bedroom, featuring a trunk he used in his travels. Across the hall is Charles Brown's bedroom. Little of their original furniture survives, but the furniture in these rooms is of the period.

Down the hall, Fanny Brawne's bedroom displays memorabilia from her life. Opposite this room is the Time Line Room, which features an interesting poster comparing various events in literary history to events in Keats's life. Poetry books are stacked near some chairs, encouraging the visitor to read and linger. The room also has several of Fanny's possessions, including a lock of her hair and the engagement ring Keats gave her. Fanny wore it until she died, even though after several years of mourning Keats, she eventually married another man.

In the same display with the ring is a tiny gold lute brooch, strung with strands of hair taken from Keats's head after he died. The lute is symbolic of lyric poetry. This symbol is also carved on Keats's tombstone in Rome, with several of the lute strings broken.

Take note of the small cupboard in the hallway. The cupboard contains a lead sink, which collected rainwater from a gutter in the roof. This provided water in the house for the residents. (This floor also contains a public toilet.)

GETTING THERE

By train: Take the Silverlink Metro to Hampstead Heath station. From there it's a three minute walk. Outside of the rail station, turn right onto South End Road and then left onto Keats Grove. Keats House will be on the left.

By Underground: Take the Northern line (Edgware branch) to the Hampstead station. It's about a 1/2 walk to Keats House from the station. Out of the Underground station, turn east on Hampstead High Street and walk downhill.

Turn left onto Downshire Hill. When you come to a Y in the road, turn right onto Keats Grove. Keats House is on the right.

From Belsize Park Underground station (also on the Northern line), it's also about a half-mile walk to Keats House, but some is uphill. Out of the Belsize Park Underground station, turn right onto Haverstock Hill. Then turn right onto Pond Street, left onto South End Road, and left onto Keats Grove. Keats House will be on the left.

By bus: Numbers 24, 46, 168, or C11, all go to South End Green, stopping next to Hampstead Heath train station. From there it's a three minute walk. Walk down South End Road and turn onto Keats Grove. Alternatively, bus # 268 stops at the corner of Rosslyn Hill and Downshire Hill. From there, walk down Downshire Hill, bear right onto Keats Grove and Keats House will be on the right.

PLACES TO EAT
There is no café in the house, but there are lots of pubs and restaurants in Hampstead. The Freemasons Pub is nearby on Downshire Hill.

WORKS BY KEATS
Poems—1817
Endymion—1818
Lamia—1820

RELATED SITES TO VISIT
Victoria & Albert Museum, London (www.victoria andalbert. org.uk): View the sketch of Keats by Severn. The nearest Underground station is South Kensington on the Piccadilly, Circle, and District lines.

National Portrait Gallery, London (www.npg.org.uk): View the painting *Keats Reading* by Severn. Several other sketches by Keats and of Keats are in the collection but not on regular display. Underground Stop: Charing Cross Station on the Northern line, or Leicester Square on the Piccadilly line

Keats-Shelley House, Rome (www.keats-shelley-house. org): In 1906, the Keats-Shelley Memorial Association bought the house in Rome where Keats died. In addition to visiting the house, next to the Spanish Steps at Number 26 Piazza di Spagna, interested visitors can rent a first-floor apartment for up to six months.

ARMCHAIR TRAVELING

www.john-keats.com
www.keats-shelley.co.uk

Keats-Shelley Association of America
Room 226, The New York Public Library
476 Fifth Avenue
New York, NY 10018-2788

FURTHER READING

John Keats by Robert Gittings, 1968 (considered by many to be the definitive biography of Keats)

Keats by Andrew Motion, 2001 (comprehensive biography of Keats)

John Keats edited by Elizabeth Cook, 2001 (collected works of Keats, including most of his poetry and some of his letters)

Chapter Nine

BATEMAN'S

Home of Rudyard Kipling, 1902–1936

The magic, you see, lies in a ring or fence that you take refuge in.

Rudyard Kipling, *Something of Myself*

There's something about the atmosphere at Bateman's that makes you want to settle in and never leave. The views of the rolling farmlands of the Sussex countryside are beautiful, of course, but it's the house that invites you to stay. Kipling himself felt the same way when he first saw it.

Kipling was born in India on December 30, 1865. He was named Rudyard after Lake Rudyard in Staffordshire, where his parents met. His father was a sculptor and professor of architectural sculpture.

The family lived in India until Rudyard was six. His parents then left him with an English couple in Portsmouth who took in children of British people living in India. Rudyard was verbally and physically abused by the wife and son, but he quickly learned what was necessary to escape their punishments. Finally, his mother rescued him from this grim situation.

He went to college, but he wasn't academic enough for university, so his father found a job for him in what is now Pakistan. Rudyard became the assistant editor of a small newspaper, where he developed his writing ability and began to write short stories for the paper. A collection of these was published in his first book, *Plain Tales from the Hills*. He was 22. The next year, he published six more books of short stories.

Rudyard decided to move to London, then the literary capital of the world. He returned via the United States and Canada, where he traveled extensively and was excited that he got to meet Mark Twain.

He married Caroline "Carrie" Balestier, the sister of his American publisher, on January 18, 1892. Henry James gave away the bride. They married in London, and headed off for their honeymoon to America and Japan. Carrie was American and they decided to live in America, so they settled in Vermont in 1893. Kipling had a public, rather scandalous, fight with Carrie's brother, and the couple moved back to England in 1896.

Kipling had been wandering the world most of his life, and now he needed a refuge. He first settled in a home called The Elms in the village of Rottingdean, near Brighton, but he was frequently bothered by sightseers who wanted a glimpse of the famous man. More urgently, he was devastated by the death of his daughter Josephine from pneumonia. (He'd written the *Just So Stories* for her.)

So when he and Carrie first saw Bateman's, Kipling said it was "a real House in which to settle down for keeps." They bought Bateman's in 1902. It included a mill and 33 acres of land, but the house had no electricity or bathrooms. Still, he and Carrie, along with their son, John, and daughter Elsie, moved into Bateman's. They began extensive renovations on the house and outbuildings.

Kipling also spent a lot of money acquiring parcels of land surrounding Bateman's, eventually amounting to about three hundred acres. This not only preserved the original Bateman's estate but created an additional buffer of privacy around his life.

Kipling relished becoming a landowner. He threw himself into the experience. The work helped him fight off the long bouts of depression he'd been prone to throughout his life. And while he directed the renovation of the house and grounds, he wrote. Most of his work from this time was inspired by the house and the gardens.

The story "A Doctor of Medicine," from *Rewards and Fairies*, is set in the mulberry garden. There, a young brother and sister meet Puck, who fascinates them with his stories of the history of England. The timeless poem "If—" was first published in *Rewards and Fairies*.

In 1907, Kipling became the first Englishman, and youngest person ever, to win the Nobel Prize in Literature. He used the money to create the rose garden at Bateman's.

Kipling was quite a humorous man, frequently telling funny stories to his friends and children. He would read his own stories to his children, frequently laughing uncontrollably at his own jokes. When his death was incorrectly announced in a magazine, he wrote to them: "I've just read that I am dead. Don't forget to delete me from your list of subscribers."

Over the years leading up to WWI, Kipling had many visitors to the house and seemed to enjoy their company. His friends, numerous relatives, and fellow writers such as Henry James and Rider Haggard were invited to lunch or to stay over. A privileged few were invited into his study.

Sadness hit again when his son, John, was killed during WWI. Kipling and Carrie consoled themselves by reading Jane Austen. Kipling frequently read out loud to Carrie and Elsie. This may be the inspiration for his story "The Janeites," which tells the tale of soldiers during the war who belonged to a secret society called the Janeites. To help them deal with the horrors of war, they read Jane Austen. After the war, the hero continues to read Austen, declaring, "There's no one to touch Jane when you're in a tight place."

As the years went by, Kipling continued to have bouts of

depression and illness that slowed him down more and more. This coincides with the decline of the popularity of his work. He died of a perforated ulcer on January 18, 1936. He was 70 years old.

Carrie left Bateman's to the National Trust when she died in 1939, saving it as a memorial to her husband. It probably has more furniture and personal possessions intact than any of the other homes featured in this book.

VISITING BATEMAN'S

Burwash, Etchingham
East Sussex TN19 7DS
Phone: (0)1435 882302
www.nationaltrust.org.uk (search for Bateman's)
Hours: Mid-March to late October, Saturday to Wednesday, 11:00 a.m.–5:00 p.m.

> December, open first three weekends only; downstairs rooms decorated in traditional Edwardian Christmas style.

> Garden/tea room/shop: open Mid-March to late October, Saturday to Wednesday, 10:00 a.m.–5:00 p.m.

> Gift shop/tea room is open (although with limited hours) in November, December, and March, even when the house is not open.

> The mill grinds corn most Wednesdays and Saturdays at 2:00 p.m.

Admission: adults £8.60; concessions for children, families, and groups

Free to members of National Trust.

Wheelchair access: A drop-off point is on site. Two manual wheelchairs are available. Entry has one step but ramp is available. Ground floor has steps. There is no access to other floors, but a virtual tour of upper floors is available. There are steps to the shop entrance and the tea room entrance.

Gift shop.

The date 1634 carved in stone over the front door sets the stage for a home that Kipling filled with furnishings from that period. The staircases and paneling are carved from local oak trees, many from the original structure, others added during Kipling's remodeling. The building is constructed of local sandstone, and the chimneys and roof tiles are made from local clay. All in all, these individual elements combine to form a solid structure that provided the stability and refuge that Kipling needed.

Next to the front door is a bell-pull that Kipling described in his autobiography, *Something of Myself*, as a talisman of the happiness that he felt the house provided. It had originally hung outside the home of his aunt Georgiana Macdonald, whose home he visited in childhood. A painting of that home, The Grange, hangs inside the entry hall.

Upstairs is Kipling's study. Docents frequently stop here to relate stories about Kipling and his writing habits. The desk at which he wrote is still as he left it, with many of his talismans on it, as they were when he was working. They include a canoe-shaped pen tray, a paperweight, and a pewter inkwell. He scratched the titles of his books on the inkwell. Although his typewriter is on display, he rarely used it because, he claimed, it couldn't spell. But his secretary used it to type his stories from his handwritten manuscripts.

Kipling would lie on the daybed, smoking and thinking about his writing. When the muse hit him, he would jump up and go to the desk to continue his writing.

The walls of the study are filled with books, including not only classics but books about India, the history of England, and Sussex history in particular, as well as books on farm management.

A painting of Carrie Kipling hangs over the fireplace. Rudyard designed the Rose Garden at Bateman's, and his original design hangs on the wall here as well.

A small guest bedroom is next on the tour, and a larger bedroom is now an exhibition room, with the Nobel Prize being the highlight of the room. The certificate has an English translation next to it.

Be sure to take a peek into the Powder Closet, which reveals the explanation for the modern-day term "powder room." When it was fashionable for men to wear wigs, they would go to a small room like this to powder the wigs.

Back downstairs, you can tour the dining room. Dining was a formal occasion and the Kiplings always 'dressed' for dinner, even when it was just family. Furnishings include a beautiful set of Chippendale chairs and an embroidered fire screen.

Across the hall is a sitting room used by the Kiplings' daughter Elsie. In earlier days, it was used as a schoolroom for Elsie and her brother, John, who died during World War I. A scene from a story in *Puck of Pook's Hill* is set here. A bronze bust of Kipling can be seen in this room.

Be sure to leave plenty of time to explore the gardens. The views over the Sussex Weald are much as they were in Kipling's day. The rectangular pond on the southwest side of the house was where Kipling would frequently take guests in a paddleboat. He delighted in noting in his visitor's book that certain guests FIP (Fell in Pond). This pond and the rose garden were built with the money Kipling received for his Nobel Prize in 1907.

A wild garden leads the way down to the river and the mill. Shortly after moving into Bateman's, Kipling disconnected the old mill grinder and installed a waterwheel, which generated enough electricity to provide four hours of light every night in the house. The grounds down to the River Dudwell contain roses, wildflowers, fruit, and herbs.

Kipling loved driving in the countryside, and he kept notes of his excursions. To him, driving was an adventure. His first Rolls-Royce is on display in the garage.

PLACES TO EAT

Bateman's Tea Room has outside tables when the weather's good. There's a picnic area adjacent to the car park.

GETTING THERE

By train: Etchingham train station is about three miles away. Call for a taxi from the station. Or take the bus, below.

By bus: Renown Coach line stops outside the Etchingham train station. Take # 318 bus towards Uckfield. Get off at the Burwash stop. Then it's a ten minute walk to Bateman's down Bateman's Lane. (No buses on Sundays.)

By car: Bateman's is half a mile south of Burwash. Take the A265 west from Burwash, then take the first turn on the left onto Bateman's Lane. It's about 1/2 mile from there.

WORKS BY KIPLING
The Story of the Gadsbys—1888
Plain Tales from the Hills—1888
The Phantom Rickshaw and other Eerie Tales—1888
The Light That Failed—1890
Mandalay (poetry)—1890)
Gunga Din (poetry)—1890
The Jungle Book (short stories)—1894
The Second Jungle Book (short stories)—1895
"If—" (poetry)—1895
Captains Courageous—1897
"Recessional"—1897
The Day's Work—1898
Stalky & Co.—1899
"The White Man's Burden"—1899
Kim—1901
Just So Stories—1902
Puck of Pook's Hill—1906
Life's Handicap (short stories)—1915
Something of Myself (autobiography)—1937

RELATED SITES
Westminster Abbey, London (www.westminster-abbey.org): Kipling's ashes are buried in Poet's Corner.
   The Grange in Rottingdean (www.visitbrighton.com): Kipling's study while living at the Elms is re-created at the **Grange Museum and Art Gallery**. Free admission. High Street, Rottingdean, East Sussex. Phone: (0) 1273 301004

ARMCHAIR TRAVELING
   www.kipling.org.uk is the web site of the Kipling Society.
   www.burwash.org has great information on the village of Burwash.

FURTHER READING

Rudyard Kipling—His Life and Work by Charles Carrington, 1970

Something of Myself and Other Autobiographical Writings edited by Thomas Pinney, 1991

The Unforgiving Minute, A Life of Rudyard Kipling by Harry Ricketts, 1999

Chapter Ten

Lamb House

Home of Henry James, 1898–1916
Home of E. F. Benson, 1919–1940

*L*amb House seems to attract writers. Or perhaps it inspires them. In addition to Henry James and E. F. Benson, it has been home Rumer Godden (1964–1967), biographer H. Montgomery Hyde (1963–1967), and Sir Brian Batsford, who designed dust jackets for travel books in the 1930s. Writers as diverse as Beatrix Potter, Edith Wharton, and H. G. Wells have visited the residents of Lamb House.

The house is named for James Lamb, who built it in 1723. Its first claim to fame was when King George I was forced by a storm to leave his ship and seek refuge in Rye in 1726. The owners of Lamb House gave the king their finest bedroom, which was, of course, their own. Mrs. Lamb was pregnant, and on the first night of the king's visit, she gave birth to a baby boy.

The king graciously consented to be godfather, and the parents (rather wisely) named the baby George. Later, the bedroom where King George had slept would be called the King's Room and used as a guest room by Henry James.

Old, square, red-roofed, well assured of its right to the place it took up in the world . . .

Henry James, *The Awkward Age*

Although Lamb House served as inspiration in *The Awkward Age* and *The Turn of the Screw*, most of James's novels focus on the larger world of society. He was an expert at showing the reader what people really thought behind their polite masks, even though the other characters in the novel may not see it. His early work depicted the innocents of America being exposed to the corrupt society of Europe. Later, as James himself became disenchanted with society, his novels reflected this.

Born on April 15, 1843, to a prominent American family, Henry James spent his young-adult years traveling through Europe. When he returned to Boston in 1870, he found it stifling and provincial. He attended Harvard Law School but gave this up, as he always knew he wanted to write.

He had written some travel pieces during his tour of Europe and sold them to such magazines as *Atlantic Monthly* and *Nation*. They chronicled the adventures of Americans in Europe and were later collected into a book called *Transatlantic Sketches*. After leaving Harvard, he began a novel that he hoped would earn him enough money to return to Europe. This was eventually to become his first book, *Watch and Ward*.

The next several years were filled with a long trip to Italy, followed by short stints in New York and Boston. During this time, he wrote numerous travel sketches, wrote book and art reviews, and worked on novels, but he longed for Europe. In 1875, he went to live in Paris but tired of it after a year.

In 1876, he went to London and felt he had finally found the country he wanted to live in for the rest of his life. Wandering around the world had become tiresome, and he longed for a refuge. He found it in 1895 when he saw a watercolor sketch of the Garden Room at Lamb House. This ivy-covered brick structure had been built next to the main house by James Lamb in 1743. It featured a gorgeous bow window that looked out onto West Street. Enchanted by the sketch, James made a point of going to Rye to see the house, and he fell in love with it. Two years later, the owner died, and James signed a 21-year lease on the house. Two years after moving in, he bought it outright for £2,000.

When Henry James found Lamb House, he had realized it was the house of his dreams, yet moving into this house brought with it some ambivalence about settling down and giving up his nomadic life. He worked out these feelings in *The Turn of the Screw*, a ghost story set in a house called Bly. There's a description in that novel of a dining room opening onto a garden, much like the dining room in Lamb House does.

Moving to the country also meant James was cut off from London society. He kept a flat in the Chelsea area of London but spent more and more time in Rye. He began to rely on telegrams to communicate with his friends, which may have inspired his story "In the Cage," which relates the tale of a girl whose life revolves around her job in a post office. She lives vicariously through the telegrams she handles for the residents of Mayfair.

To help him cope with loneliness and the strain of feeling cut off from London life, James invited numerous friends and relatives to visit. The first was his nephew, Henry James, son of his brother William. Henry James Junior, as he became known, would inherit Lamb House on his uncle's death and later bequeath it to the National Trust.

Another early guest was A. C. Benson, Master of Magdalene College, Cambridge, and author of the lyrics to "Land of Hope and Glory." A. C.'s brother, E. F. Benson, also visited and later recalled hearing James dictating to his typist in the Garden Room. Perhaps this planted the seed that he would one day live in Lamb House himself.

When guests arrived by train, James would send his gardener with a wheelbarrow to fetch their luggage for the long walk up the hill. Visitors were enchanted with the medieval town of Rye and with Lamb House, which was backed by a lovely walled garden.

In the winter, James used the Green Room (not open to the public) as his writing room. In the summer, he preferred the Garden Room. James spent many hours writing there, dictating the manuscripts of *The Wings of the Dove*, *The Ambassadors*, and *The Golden Bowl*. Sadly, the Garden Room was destroyed during World War II and has never been replaced. Close to 200 books that belonged to James were lost in the bombing.

Although he was an American by birth, James loved living in Lamb House so much that he decided to take British citizenship in 1915. Not long after, however, he went to London to visit a heart specialist and had two strokes there. He died on February 28, 1916, in his Chelsea flat. His ashes are interred with other members of his family at Cambridge Cemetery in Massachusetts.

> *"Georgie, a dream," whispered Lucia, as they stood on the doorstep waiting for their ring to be answered. "That wonderful chimney, do you see, all crooked. The church, the cobbles, the grass and dandelions growing in between them . . .*
>
> E. F. Benson,- *Mapp and Lucia*

Most readers would consider the styles of Henry James and Edward Frederic Benson to be worlds apart. James once remarked that there was no sense in using one word when five would do. Benson's stories, in contrast, move along quite swiftly.

Both writers, however, enjoyed exposing people who hid behind masks. James did it in a dramatic, often tragic, way. Benson's style was usually humorous. He seemed to delight in deflating the egos of snobs and gossips, but he wasn't above poking fun at himself as well. For example, in *Trouble for Lucia*, Lucia, who has recently been elected mayor, is discussing the protocol for the mayoral banquet. She compares herself to Queen Victoria, with Georgie Pillson as her prince consort. Georgie states that he has researched this question and that when Queen Victoria opened Parliament, Prince Albert sat beside her on the throne. Lucia replies, "I wonder if that is so. Some of those lives of the Queen are very inaccurate." Benson had published a biography of the queen four years earlier.

Edward Frederic Benson, one of six children, was born on July 14, 1867. His father was handpicked by Prince Albert to be the first headmaster of the Wellington School. Later, E. F.'s father became the first Bishop of Truro, and then the Archbishop of Canterbury. Fred (as his family called him) thoroughly enjoyed the high society and royal connections that were perks of his father's work, including living at Lambeth Palace in London. But Fred also sensed the pretentiousness of some of the people who visited his father. He enjoyed his privacy so much that his mother, Mary Sidgwick Benson, called this attitude Fredian.

Fred attended Marlborough, a private boy's school, and later attended King's College, Cambridge, studying archeology, with a special interest in Greece. He worked on digs in Greece but settled into writing as his primary career.

In 1888, he privately printed his first book, called *Sketches from Marlborough*, about his schoolboy years. His first novel, *Dodo*, was so successful that it went into a dozen printings the first year. Benson's nickname became Dodo.

As a young adult, Fred traveled and wrote, living with his parents whenever he returned to England. He worked for the Red Cross for a time, helping Greek refugees from the Greek–Turkish wars.

By 1918, both of Benson's parents had died, and so had Henry James. Benson decided to rent Lamb House, although he lived there only on weekends. His weekdays were spent in London, at his home in 25 Brompton Square. This, coincidentally, was also the address of Lucia in *Lucia in London*. In this book, Benson beautifully contrasted the differences and similarities in the lifestyles of the people of Rye to those of the people of London.

Few of the writers covered in this book used houses and towns for inspiration as much as E. F. Benson used Lamb House and Rye in the Mapp and Lucia books. He changed the name of Rye to Tilling, taken from the Tillingham River, which runs near Rye. Lamb House itself was the inspiration for Miss Mapp's home but was called Mallards in the books, and Rye's Mermaid Street was named Porpoise Street. Everyone who lived in Rye, or even visited that town, knew Tilling was Rye, however.

In 1920, Benson gave up his London flat and stayed in Rye permanently. From 1922, his brother Arthur lived with him, until Arthur died in 1925.

Benson so much enjoyed life in the small town of Rye that he became mayor for three terms. He also paid for the renovation of the church organ, just as Lucia did.

He died in London on February 29, 1940, of cancer.

VISITING LAMB HOUSE

Administered by the National Trust
West Street, Rye
East Sussex TN31 7ES
Phone: (0)1580 762334
www.nationaltrust.org.uk (search for Lamb House)
Hours: Mid-March through mid-October, Tuesdays and Saturdays only, 2:00 p.m.–6:00 p.m.
   Closed: Mid-October through mid-March
Admission: adults £4.30; concessions to children, families, and groups.
   Free to members of the National Trust.
Short guided tours are available for groups of 10 or more but must be booked in advance.
The widow of Henry James's nephew donated Lamb House to the National Trust in 1950. There are limited visiting hours because the house is occupied by a tenant. Only the first floor and garden are open to the public.

Pay at the small table right inside the entry. The morning room is on the left, and the second room on the left is the dining room. Both have French windows opening out into the garden, although visitors may enter the garden only through the dining room windows. Both rooms have fireplaces bordered by Dutch tiles, which Henry James had installed.

The morning room features a large painting of King George I over the fireplace. It also has a watercolor sketch by Beatrix Potter depicting West Street as seen from the parlor.

The room off the right of the entrance hall is called the Telephone Room, as James was one of the first people in England to have a telephone. It was also used as a writing room by

James, as well as by his guests. (Lucia moved Miss Mapp's unacceptable piano to the Telephone Room.) It's filled with first editions by James and Benson, as well as with books from their personal libraries. The room also features James's French writing desk, two Chippendale chairs, and a Sheraton side table. Also on display is a replica of a bust of James by Derwent Wood, the original of which is in the Tate Gallery.

The original lease for the house, signed by James, is framed and hung in the entrance hall. The great size of this piece of paper amazes visitors. Also in the hall are armchairs that belonged to James. In the entrance hall too, H. G. Wells recalled there being a large number of hats and walking sticks— James loved to walk and had a variety of hats for various purposes. He wore a brown felt hat when walking to the harbor and a grey hat with a black band for afternoon calling. He wore a deerstalker when he was heading to the golf club. He didn't golf but loved to have tea at the club.

The Lamb House garden is the largest private garden in Rye. Henry James's friend Alfred Parsons created it. Although James enjoyed the garden, he left the actual decisions and work to his gardener, George Gammon. Gammon won prizes at local flower shows, and James attended the shows out of respect for his gardener. One of his favorite plants, Campsis radicans, still survives today—along the right wall as the visitor exits the house through the dining room doors.

Benson's gardener was named Gabriel. Benson created the Secret Garden described in *Mapp and Lucia* from a plot of land that Henry James had bought adjacent to the garden. He placed in the garden a marble bust of the Roman Emperor Augustus, a replica of one in the British Museum. He did some of his writing here or read in the garden when the weather was fine.

This is one of my favorite gardens in England. The walls give a wonderful sense of privacy, and the herbaceous borders add a typical English cottage garden exuberance to the space. I also like the private walkway that's been created along the walls.

The back right corner of the garden contains a shady spot devoted to the graves of the dogs of Henry James and E. F. Benson.

GETTING THERE

By train: From London: Trains leave from Charing Cross station hourly with a change in Ashford (total journey time is 1hour, 45 minutes) or Hastings (total time 2 hours).

From Gatwick Airport: Change at Hastings for Rye (total journey time is about two hours).

Lamb House is about ten minutes' walk from Rye's train station, partly uphill. To walk from the train station, go straight up Market Road, then turn right onto High Street, then left onto West Street. Lamb House is at the corner of West Street and Mermaid Street. Alternatively, there are sometimes taxis at the train station.

By car: From London/M25, take the M20 to J10 and the A2070. When arriving in Rye, follow signs to Rye's main car park, Gibbet Marsh. Note that there are several cobblestone streets in Rye, all of which have limited car access and very few parking areas. It's advisable to park in one of the car parks near the train station or by the Strand Quay near the Tourist Information Centre and walk to Lamb House from there.

PLACES TO EAT

The Landgate Bistro (www.landgatebistro.co.uk): 5/6 Landgate, Rye. (0)1797 222829 This is widely considered the best restaurant in Rye.

Ypres Castle Inn (www.yprescastleinn.co.uk): For an atmospheric pub, this is the place to go. The Gun Garden is open for dining in good weather.

BOOKS PUBLISHED BY HENRY JAMES

James wrote 22 novels, 20 plays, and numerous short stories and novellas. Here is just a selection:

Watch and Ward (first novel published)—1871
Daisy Miller—1879
Washington Square—1880
Portrait of a Lady—1881
The Bostonians—1886
The Turn of the Screw—1898
A Great Good Place—1900
In the Cage—1898

The Wings of the Dove—1902
The Ambassadors—1903
The Golden Bowl—1904
The Outcry—1911
Autobiography: *A Small Boy and Others*—1913
Notes of a Son and Brother—1914
The Middle Years—1917

BOOKS PUBLISHED BY E. F. BENSON

Benson was the author of more than 100 books but is best
remembered for his Mapp and Lucia novels and his supernatural stories. Here is just a selection:
Dodo—1893
Queen Lucia—1920
Miss Mapp—1922
Lucia in London—1927
Mapp and Lucia—1931
Lucia's Progress (titled *Worshipful Lucia* in the US edition)—1935
Trouble for Lucia—1939
Secret Lives (not a Mapp and Lucia tale)—1932
Nonfiction:
Charlotte Bronte—1932
Queen Victoria—1935
The Daughters of Queen Victoria—1939
Our Family Affairs—1920
As We Were—A Victorian Peep-Show—1930
As We Are—A Modern Revue—1932
Final Edition (published after his death in 1940)

RELATED SITES TO VISIT

National Portrait Gallery, London (www.npg.co.uk), has
a portrait of Henry James by J. S. Sargent. The nearest Underground station is Charing Cross on the Northern or Bakerloo
lines, or Leicester Square on the Piccadilly line.

A Walking Tour of Mapp and Lucia's Rye: The Tilling
Society sponsors a guided walk in Rye on Wednesdays and the
first and third Saturdays of each month from April to October,

for everything you wanted to know about Mapp and Lucia—where they lived in the books as well as in the television series. The walk starts at the Hilder's Cliff Belvedere on the eastern end of High Street, overlooking Romney Marsh, and lasts about 1 1/2 hours. For more information, call (0) 1797-223114.

Rye Tourist Information Centre (www.visitrye.co.uk): On the Strand Quay in Rye. Phone (0)1797 226696

Rye Church: E. F. Benson donated the West Window of Rye Church, dedicated to his parents. He designed it himself and included portraits of his collie, Taffy, and his manservant Charlie Tomlin as a shepherd, as well as himself in mayoral robes. He also included a window commemorating his brother Arthur.

Rye Cemetery: E. F. Benson is buried here, about a half mile outside of Rye.

Cambridge, MA, USA: Henry James was cremated but has a gravestone in a cemetery in Cambridge, Massachusetts.

Westminster Abbey, London: (www.westminster-abbey.org) There's also a memorial to Henry James in Westminster Abbey, in the Poet's Corner.

ARMCHAIR TRAVELING

www.mockingbird.creighton.edu/english/HJS/home.html is a web site for the Henry James Society.

www.efbensonsociety.org is the web site for the E. F. Benson Society, which was founded in 1985. Mail can be sent to The Old Coach House, High Street, Rye, East Sussex, TN31 7JF

www.efbenson.co.uk is a fan web site with all things Bensonian.

www.friendsoftilling.com is a web site devoted to Mapp and Lucia.

www.visitrye.co.uk for information on visiting Rye.

FOR FURTHER READING

The Life of Henry James by Leon Edel (5 volumes), 1953–1972

Henry James: The Imagination of Genius by Fred Kaplan, 1992

Henry James: A Life in Letters edited by Philip Horne, 1999

The Life of E. F. Benson by Brian Masters, 1991

E. F. Benson Remembered, and the World of Tilling by Cynthia and Tony Reavell, 1991

E. F. Benson As He Was by Geoffrey Palmer, 1988

The Story of Lamb House by H. Hyde Montgomery, 1966

Chapter Eleven

Monk's House

Home of Virginia Woolf, 1919–1941

The house had lost its shelter.

Virginia Woolf, *Between the Acts*

Although Virginia Woolf is widely known as a member of the literary circle known as the Bloomsbury Group, which was centered in London, she also had a home during the last 22 years of her life in a tiny village near the East Sussex town of Lewes. Many of her later works, especially her posthumously published novel, *Between the Acts*, drew extensively on this area.

Adeline Virginia Stephen was born January 25, 1882. She had an older sister, Vanessa, and two brothers, Thoby and Adrian. Both of their parents had been married before, and the four children from those marriages lived with them in the Kensington area of London. The family spent their summers in Devon and Cornwall, and Virginia's happiest childhood memories seem to be from these holidays in the town of St. Ives. Woolf's novel *To the Lighthouse* was based on St. Ives, although in the book, the setting was the Isle of Skye.

Her father was editor of the *Dictionary of National Biography* and edited *Cornhill Magazine*. Virginia's father encouraged her to read extensively from his own library, and she spent a large part of her childhood doing just this. Her parents were very social, but Virginia was shy and hated parties. She preferred to be home reading.

Her teenage years were punctuated by several devastating losses. Her mother died when Virginia was 13. She dealt with this loss by retreating for a while into an inner world where she could avoid facing reality. Eventually she came out of it, as Stella, her half sister from her mother's first marriage, took over as female head of the household, but within a couple of years, Stella married and, sadly, died.

Virginia's father died in 1904, leading to another breakdown for Virginia. After this, the children left Kensington and moved to the Bloomsbury area of London. Although they were not, strictly speaking, children any longer, it would have been unusual for a young family to live alone without a mature adult to head the household. This was the early basis for the Bloomsbury Group.

Virginia's brother Thoby, while at Cambridge, had formed a group of friends who talked about literature, art, and politics. Now he brought his friends to the house in Bloomsbury, where they continued their lively discussions every Thursday evening, with Vanessa and Virginia acting as hostesses. Unlike the parties of their parents' time, these were casual affairs, centered on stimulating discussions rather than social niceties, and Virginia enjoyed them. The changes in their lives over the past year were a strain on Virginia, however, and in 1905, she had another nervous breakdown. To recover, the family decided to go to Greece for a holiday. There, Thoby contracted typhoid and died, another blow to Virginia.

Vanessa married Clive Bell in 1907. Over the next few years, their circle expanded to include artists like Duncan Grant and Roger Fry, writers like E. M. Forster, and the economist John Maynard Keynes. Virginia remained reserved during the discussions that took place, but she and Vanessa were treated like equals, an unusual way to treat women at the time. But, of course, times were changing.

One of the members of the group was Leonard Woolf, whom Virginia married in 1912. In 1915, Virginia published her first book, *The Voyage Out*. It was not a great success, but reviews were encouraging, and Virginia continued writing.

In that same year, she and Leonard moved out of Bloomsbury to a house called Hogarth in Richmond. One day, they found an old printing press and decided to buy it. Thus began their publishing business, which was centered in their Richmond house and therefore called the Hogarth Press.

The publishing business was a success from the beginning, and Leonard and Virginia worked at it diligently, setting type, cutting boards, and even buying the cover paper during their trips abroad. Although they worked hard, they looked on publishing as a hobby because they found the whole process interesting and fun.

They had rented a country house called Asheham near the town of Lewes in Sussex, but when it was needed for an industrial plant, they bought Monk's House in the tiny village of Rodmell.

Monk's House was in a sad state of disrepair when the Woolfs bought it, and over the years, they renovated and expanded it. The garden, in particular, was one of the features that attracted the Woolfs to the house. Leonard enjoyed gardening so much that in *Who's Who*, he listed his hobbies as printing and gardening. The couple traveled extensively and brought back furnishings and artwork for the house and statuary for the garden.

Meanwhile, their publishing business had outgrown the house in Richmond, so in 1924, they returned to Bloomsbury. They rented a house in Tavistock Square, which was to become their London home, with the publishing business in the basement.

Virginia established her own office in this house, where she would write for several hours every morning. She worked the rest of the day in the printing business or walked the streets of London. Her long walks gave her inspiration for her stories, such as the London scenes in *Mrs. Dalloway*.

When at Rodmell, she did her morning writing at the Lodge, a small building at the back of the garden. After finishing her daily output of writing, she spent the rest of the day walking in the countryside around the village. Her writing career supplied the money needed to refurbish the house.

Virginia's life was plagued with continuing bouts of illness, including migraine headaches so severe that she couldn't write for weeks at a time. Being unable to write was almost as painful to her as the headaches.

As the World War II approached and London was bombed, Virginia and Leonard spent more and more time in Rodmell. Because Rodmell was located in southern England, near the Channel, however, it was just as vulnerable to air raids as London was. Virginia worked on her last novel, *Between the Acts*, the plot of which seemed to be a metaphor for the time between the two great wars. It also seemed to reflect the growing realization that even the tiny village and cottage where she had sought sanctuary were no longer safe.

Carrying on became a way of life, and Virginia seemed to be as anxious to survive the war as any other British citizen, yet in the midst of war, in 1941, she took her own life, walking into the river near Rodmell with stones in her pockets. Her body wasn't found for two weeks. Her ashes were scattered in the garden of Rodmell.

Virginia's suicide note to Leonard explained that the voices in her head were overtaking her once again and she knew she couldn't recover from them this time. Decades later, however, the voices in her novels, short stories, and essays still speak to readers.

VISITING MONK'S HOUSE
Administered by the National Trust
Rodmell
Lewes, East Sussex BNJ 3HF

Phone: (0)1323 870001
www.nationaltrust.org.uk (search for Monk's House)
Hours: late March to late October, Wednesdays and Satur-
    days, 2:00 p.m.–5:30 p.m.
Admission: Adults £4.20, concessions to children and families
    Free to members of the National Trust.
Discount for groups over 10 people, but must book one
month ahead

Leonard left the house to their friend Mrs. Parsons, who
left it to the National Trust. As in Virginia's day, the front door
is never used. Visitors enter at the back of the house.

The house is full of the arts and crafts of Virginia's friends
and her sister, Vanessa. Their friend Duncan Grant, along with
Vanessa, painted the table in the large sitting room. Many of
the tiles here and throughout the house were painted by Duncan or Vanessa.

In the dining room are more examples of the artistic talents
of Vanessa and Duncan. They designed all the dining room
chairs and the music cabinet. Duncan Grant's mother did the
gorgeous needlework framing a mirror. Personal touches can
be seen, as in the collection of walking sticks and the set of
woods used to play bowls on the outside lawn, a favorite pas-
time of the Woolfs.

Virginia's most enduring nonfiction book is probably *A
Room of One's Own*. Her main theme in this book is that a
woman must have money and a room of her own if she is to
write. This conviction was reflected in her insistence on adding
a writing studio to Monk's House in 1929. In the end, however,
this room didn't suit her as a writing room, so she used it as a
bedroom and continued to do her writing in the Lodge at the
back of the garden. The tiles around the bedroom fireplace
were painted by Vanessa and depict a lighthouse surrounded by
a deep blue sea, possibly alluding to Virginia's book *To the Lighthouse*.

Virginia spent several hours every day writing in the Lodge.
Originally, this structure was closer to the house, but it was later
moved beyond the apple orchard and a brick path was added so
she could access it easily in all kinds of weather. Although not

open to the public, the door to the Lodge is open so visitors can get a peek into Woolf's writing sanctuary. Much larger than in Virginia's time, the Lodge today still holds her desk and the blue writing paper that she used. Photographs taken by Virginia and Leonard are also on display in the entryway to the Lodge.

Leonard planted a vegetable garden and the apple orchard that survive today. Virginia's short story "The Orchard" uses the apple orchard at Monk's House as inspiration. Old millstones from a previous family of millers line the path. Virginia and Leonard's ashes are scattered in the field beyond the garden.

GETTING THERE

By train: From London Victoria to the Lewes train station. From the Lewes train station it's four miles to Monk's House. Take a taxi from the Lewes train station or the bus (below).

By bus: Renown Coach Line operates bus #123 from Lewes train station or Lewes bus station. Take the bus towards Newhaven and get off at the Rodmell (Abergavenny Arms) stop. Follow signs to Monk's House, about a 1/2 mile walk.

By car: Take the A27 southwest of Lewes. Follow the signs for Kingston and then for Rodmell Village. Once in the village, turn left at the Abergavenny Arms pub. Monk's House is one half mile on the right. There is a small free parking lot, but no room for coaches, which must discharge passengers in the village, who must walk from there.

WORKS BY WOOLF

The Voyage Out—1915
Night and Day—1919
Jacob's Room—1922
Mrs. Dalloway—1925
The Common Reader—1925
To the Lighthouse—1927
Orlando—1928
A Room of One's Own—1929
The Waves—1931
Flush: A Biography—1933

The Years—1937
Roger Fry—A Biography—1940
Between the Acts—1941

RELATED SITES TO VISIT

Charleston (www.charleston.org.uk): This is the country home of Vanessa Bell and Duncan Grant and was visited extensively and decorated by many members of the Bloomsbury Group. It is about five miles from Monk's House.

National Portrait Gallery, London (www.npg.org.uk): The gallery displays several paintings of Virginia and Leonard Woolf. It is on St. Martin's Lane near the National Gallery of Art. The nearest Underground station is Charing Cross on the Northern and Bakerloo lines, or Leicester Square on the Piccadilly line.

British Library, London (www.bl.uk): The library holds first editions of all of Woolf's novels, as well as some handwritten manuscripts, such as for *Mrs. Dalloway*. Also of interest is the only recording of Virginia Woolf's voice, available in the library's Sound Archive. The nearest Underground station is King's Cross/St. Pancras on the Piccadilly, Northern, Victoria, Circle, Metropolitan, and Hammersmith & City lines.

ARMCHAIR TRAVELING

www.utoronto.ca/IVWS is the International Virginia Woolf Society web site.

www.virginiawoolfsociety.co.uk is the web site for the Great Britain Virginia Woolf Society. This site lists numerous sources for further information about Woolf, plus links to other sites.

FURTHER READING

Virginia Woolf: A Biography by Quentin Bell, 1972, reprinted 1996
Virginia Woolf by Hermione Lee, 1996

Chapter Twelve

HARDY'S COTTAGE
and MAX GATE

Homes of Thomas Hardy

Hardy's Cottage, 1840–1874
Max Gate, 1885–1928

*It was a long, low cottage with a hipped roof of thatch, hav-
ing dormer windows breaking up into the eaves, a chimney
standing in the middle of the ridge, and another at each end.*

Thomas Hardy, *Under the Greenwood Tree*

This thatched-roof cottage, described in Hardy's second
published novel, also describes the cottage in which
he was born on June 2, 1840. It was built by Hardy's

great-grandfather in 1800, although that original cottage was much smaller than the one we see today. Hardy's pride and love for his ancestral home is apparent in his descriptions of the cottage in *Under the Greenwood Tree*. In his later years, he would frequently return to the cottage on his birthday. He'd be sharply critical of anything that looked shabby.

Hardy used his rural surroundings extensively in his books. His village of Higher Bockhampton is known in his books as Upper Mellstock, and the nearest city, Dorchester, is called Casterbridge in his books. The whole of southwestern England was called Wessex in Hardy's novels, taken from the early Saxon name for the area.

Young Thomas loved nature, and it's said that his mother once found him sleeping in his cradle with a large snake curled up beside him. This love of nature is evident in most of his stories. The first paragraph of *Under the Greenwood Tree*, for example, suggests that every tree has a voice: the holly whistles, the beech rustles. Hardy didn't just use nature *in* his writing; he sometimes used it *for* his writing: during long walks, when he found himself with an important thought but no paper on which to record it, he would jot it down on leaves, wood chips, or pieces of stone or slate that he found on the ground.

Nature is just the background for most of Hardy's writing, however. The plots of many of his novels revolve around fate. His stories frequently end on a note of hope that man will endure against fate and against nature because of his innate strength.

Music was an important part of family life for young Hardy. Like his father and grandfather before him, Thomas played the violin and sang in the church choir. So it's not surprising that his first major novel, *Under the Greenwood Tree*, begins with a church choir going door to door, singing Christmas carols on Christmas Eve.

Although he wanted to be a poet, at age 16, Hardy was apprenticed as an architect. He spent his spare time studying the classics. After six years, he moved to London and worked for an architect there but continued his study of the classics by visiting museums and reading. He tried to publish some poetry but failed. Eventually, he moved back to Dorchester for health reasons. Although he returned to his old job as an architect's assistant, he couldn't suppress his urge to write. He realized that there was a better chance of making a living with novels than with poetry, so he turned his attention to novels.

Two publishers turned down his first book, *The Poor Man and the Lady*, but he continued writing and finally published another book, *Desperate Remedies*, in 1871. It was not well received, and although he'd started another book, *Under the Greenwood Tree*, he resigned himself to architecture.

Then the publisher of *Desperate Remedies* agreed to publish *Under the Greenwood Tree* and offered Hardy the chance to do a serial for them as well. This novel, *A Pair of Blue Eyes*, was followed by *Far from the Madding Crowd*, which was serialized in *Cornhill Magazine*. *Far from the Madding Crowd* received good reviews from critics and readers. Heartened, Hardy gave up architecture and started writing full time.

Because his new career looked promising, he decided he could now marry. While working on plans to restore a church in Cornwall, he had fallen in love with the rector's sister-in-law, Emma Gifford. Thomas and Emma married in London on September 17, 1874, despite the objections of both families.

After a brief period of living in London, during which Hardy became seriously ill, the Hardys moved back to Dorset. In1885, they moved to Max Gate, a house outside of Dorchester, which Hardy designed and his father and brother built.

His first book while living at Max Gate was *The Woodlanders*. Hardy always considered it his favorite story, and it received excellent reviews.

As his fame as a writer grew, Hardy's marriage became less happy. Emma withdrew more and more, frequently staying in her room while Hardy entertained his many guests.

Next, Hardy wrote *Tess of the d'Urbervilles*, *The Mayor of Casterbridge*, and *Jude the Obscure*. This last book was greatly disliked by the public and was even subjected to a public burning. Ironically, these are the novels for which Hardy is now best known. The outrage that surrounded the publication of these books surprised Hardy, prompting him to give up novel writing and to confine himself to writing poetry.

Emma died in 1912. Two years later, Hardy married his friend and secretary, Florence Dugdale. The next years of his life were happy ones. His reputation as an author was assured, and he won numerous awards.

When Hardy died on January 11, 1928, his stature dictated that he should be buried in Poet's Corner in Westminster Abbey, but there were those who felt that because his novels demonstrated his fondness for Wessex, his heart should stay there. Accordingly, his heart was buried in a separate casket in Stinsford Churchyard, next to the grave of his first wife. His ashes were interred next to Charles Dickens in Westminster Abbey.

VISITING HARDY'S COTTAGE
Administered by the National Trust
Higher Bockhampton
Near Dorchester
Dorset, DT2 8QJ
Phone: (0)1305 262366
www.national-trust.org.uk (search for Thomas Hardy)
Hours: mid March to late October, Thursday to Monday,
        11:00 a.m.–5:00 p.m.
Admission: 4.75
Free to members of the National Trust.
Wheelchair access: A drop-off point is available for disabled visitors, but call first. There are steps to the entrance. The ground floor is mostly accessible; no access to other floors. The grounds are largely accessible.
The cottage is a 10-minute walk from car park. No coach parking.

I recommend visiting Hardy's Cottage first and then visiting Max Gate, in order to get a proper perspective on how far this writer came from his rural roots. Like Wordsworth, Hardy's birthplace was humble and charming but he built a house after his writing success that is formal and imposing.

Hardy's Cottage is a classic thatched-roof home surrounded by a charming cottage garden. An English friend of mine would call it a chocolate box garden, meaning it's worthy of being pictured on the front of a fancy chocolate box. The house is covered in vines, and the garden is jam-packed with flowers and shrubs, all creating the quintessential English cottage garden.

The parlor on the left side of the house is described in *Under the Greenwood Tree* and features a long beam bisecting the ceiling, mentioned in the Christmas Eve scene.

The tiny room off the parlor is known as the office. This is where Hardy's father and grandfather did their bookkeeping for their building business.

Upstairs, the first room belonged to Hardy's sisters, Kate and Mary. The next room is where Hardy was born.

The room of most interest on the second floor is Hardy's room. Here he would read and write, sometimes sitting on the deep window seat, gazing out the window for inspiration. It's said that he wrote *Under the Greenwood Tree* from this room.

A narrow ladder leads down to the kitchen. Those concerned about going down this steep staircase can instead return to the one on the other side of the house. The brick oven in the kitchen was used in Hardy's time for baking bread and pies.

Spend some time wandering around the garden. Absorb the atmosphere, imagining the young Hardy running past you and into the woods or enjoying tea in the garden.

I arrived at the cottage by taxi from the train station. On the way to the cottage, my driver had told me he'd been elected the Mayor of Casterbridge during the last Thomas Hardy festival. He'd given me his card and told me to call when I was finished touring the cottage and he'd come back to pick me up. Unfortunately, there was a problem with the phone at the cottage, and then when I asked the docent about a bus, the answer was "none on Sundays." He pointed me in the general direction of Dorchester, and I started walking. After all, I reminded myself, Hardy and his brother and two sisters walked to school in Dorchester every day. If they could do it, so could I.

Before I got to the end of the lane, however, a middle-aged couple drove up behind me and offered me a lift into Dorchester. I'd noticed them touring the cottage while I was there, and they mentioned that they were members of the National Trust, out for a Sunday tour. I was becoming a regular hitchhiker. Once again, kind strangers refused my offer of money for petrol and waved cheerfully after dropping me off in the center of Dorchester.

I spent an hour taking the Thomas Hardy walk around Dorchester, then walked (no hitchhiking this time) to Max Gate, a mile outside of town.

GETTING THERE

By train: Dorchester South and Dorchester West are each about four miles from Hardy's Cottage. Taxis are available at the train station.

By bus: There is weekday bus service from the train station to Hardy's Cottage: Wilts and Dorset x64. Alight at Bockhampton Lane—it's a 20-minute walk from there.

By car: Hardy's Cottage is three miles northeast of Dorchester, half a mile south of A35. From Kingston Maurward roundabout, follow the signs for Stinsford and Higher Bockhampton.

VISITING MAX GATE

Administered by the National Trust.
Alington Avenue
Near Dorchester
Dorset, DT1 2AB
Phone: (0)1305 262538
www.nationaltrust.org.uk (search for Max Gate)
Hours: early April to late September; Mondays, Wednesdays,
        and Sundays, 2:00 p.m.–5:00 p.m.
Admission: 3, child rates available.
Free to members of the National Trust.
Because tenants currently occupy Max Gate, visiting hours are limited. Also, only the entry hall, dining room, and drawing room are open for touring. Docents, however, are knowledgeable and anxious to answer questions.

Before entering Max Gate, note the sundial on the tower on the far right side of the house. This was designed by Hardy but wasn't hung until after his death. The inscription *Quid de Nocte?* means *What of the Night?*

Pay the entry fee in the hall, and then proceed to the dining room on the left. Max Gate was designed by Hardy and has a number of unusual features, such as the moveable bookcases flanking the fireplace, and the high windowsill to prevent outsiders from looking in. By the time Hardy moved here, he was already famous, and as the years went by, many sightseers would stop to see the home of Thomas Hardy.

Hardy was a friend of many famous writers of his day, some of whom visited him here at Max Gate. This room, and the drawing room, attest to this with memorabilia from T. E. Lawrence, the Prince of Wales, and Yeats, among others.

Return to the hall and cross to the drawing room, opposite. Here, in his later years, Hardy hosted tea at four o'clock, inviting famous friends such as Rudyard Kipling, Robert Louis Stevenson, H. G. Wells, Virginia Woolf, and countless others. The windows look onto the garden, which is accessible through the conservatory.

The urn in the center of the lawn belonged to Hardy. The house cat is usually wandering around, ready at any moment to have his picture taken, possibly on the same bench where Hardy had his photograph taken with the Prince of Wales.

Past the palm tree, planted by Hardy, is a wall Hardy built to keep out intruders. He had a small door built into the wall, still visible today, through which he would escape from unwanted visitors.

Featured in an alcove near the wall is the sarsen stone that was found during excavations of the lawn in 1885. Max Gate was built on an ancient stone circle dating back to 3,000 B.C. This stone is described in his poem "The Shadow on the Stone."   Following the path to the right takes visitors to the Nut Walk, where Hardy would take a morning and evening stroll. This path brings visitors back to the front of the house. Follow the path to the left of the house to see the pet cemetery, where Hardy buried his pets and even carved their headstones.

GETTING THERE

By train: Travel from London Waterloo to Dorchester South. Take a taxi from the train station to Max Gate. Note that a market takes place near the train station on Wednesdays.

The 4500-year-old Maumbury Rings are also near the train station, and occasional outdoor performances take place there during the summer.

By car: From Dorchester, follow the A352 Wareham Road to the roundabout named Max Gate, at the junction of A36 Dorchester bypass. Turn left and then left again into the cul-de-sac outside the house.

WORKS BY THOMAS HARDY

Desperate Remedies—1871
Under the Greenwood Tree—1872
Far from the Madding Crowd—1874
The Return of the Native—1878
The Trumpet-Major—1880
The Mayor of Casterbridge—1886
The Woodlanders—1887
Wessex Tales—1888
Tess of the d'Urbervilles—1891
The Well-Beloved—1892
Jude the Obscure—1895
Wessex Poems—1898

RELATED SITES

Dorset County Museum (www.dorsetcountymuseum.org): The museum is located on High West Street, Dorchester; (0)1305 262735: It displays the world's largest collection of Hardy relics. Hardy's second wife, Florence, donated the contents of his study to this museum. They've used these items to create a reconstruction of his study. The Museum is open April to October, Monday to Saturday, 10:00 a.m.–5:00 p.m.; open Tuesday to Saturday, 10:00 a.m.–4:00 p.m. for the remainder of the year. Admission fee is £6.50; concessions for seniors and children.

Sculpture of Hardy: By Eric Kennington, unveiled by James Barrie in 1931, this statue is located in Dorchester on High West Street.

The Kings Arms Hotel: On High East Street in Dorchester – this is where Michael Henchard, the mayor of Casterbridge, sold his family. **The Antelope Hotel** (on Antelope

Walk in Dorchester) is also mentioned in the *Mayor of Caster-bridge*.

Westminster Abbey, London (www.westminster-abbey.org): Hardy's ashes are buried here. The nearest Underground stop is Westminster on the District and Circle lines.

St. Michael's Church, Stinsford, near Dorchester: Hardy's heart is buried here, next to Emma's grave.

ARMCHAIR TRAVELING

www.visit-dorset.org.uk for the Dorchester Tourist Information Centre.

www.visit-dorchester.co.uk for more to do in Dorchester and accommodations. www.hardysociety.org is the web site for the Thomas Hardy Society.

FURTHER READING

The Early Life of Thomas Hardy by Florence Emily Hardy, 1928

The Later Years of Thomas Hardy, 1930. (Written mostly by Hardy himself, but not published until after his death.)

Thomas Hardy's Wessex by Hermann Lea, 1913. (Lea lived in Hardy's Cottage for 10 years after the Hardy family left it. He became a close friend of Hardy's, and Hardy lent his support to the book, providing Lea with advice on the places that inspired various scenes in his novels.)

Chapter Thirteen

GREENWAY

Home of Agatha Christie, 1938–1959

A white Georgian house of about 1780 or 90, with woods sweeping down to the Dart below, and a lot of fine shrubs and trees—the ideal house, a dream house.

Agatha Christie, *An Autobiography*

*A*gatha Christie has always been one of my favorite mystery writers, so when I heard that the gardens of Greenway, her dream house on the coast of Devon, were open to the public, I had to visit.

While touring the gardens of Greenway, I got a glimpse of what family life was like at her summer home. I could picture Christie arranging treasure hunts on the grounds for her nephews and grandson, or working out a plot while sitting in the garden looking over the River Dart.

Christie loved gardening, and Greenway's mature rhododendrons and magnolias blooming along winding woodland paths are a testament to this. Walking past the dahlia border that Christie planted, one comes across what's now called the putting green. This is where the family played a game called clock golf, an early form of miniature golf.

For the Christie family, the only annoyance on this idyllic estate was the hikers from the nearby youth hostel who came up to the house and peered in at them while they were eating lunch.

I urge you to read *Dead Man's Folly* before visiting Greenway. The main action takes place in a white Georgian house (called Nasse House in the book) set on a hill above the river. The owners are annoyed by the hikers from the nearby youth hostel who continuously trespass on the estate. The garden is described as having winding paths through the woods, bordered with magnolias and rhododendrons. Someone asks for extra putters for the clock golf that will be played during the next day's fete. The murder of young Marlene Tucker takes place in the boathouse. Several other spots in the book are also inspired by Greenway: the charming cottage by the river, the ferry, the lodge, and the battery. Finally, Nasse House was requisitioned by the army during the war, as was Greenway.

Clearly, Christie's beloved Greenway was a source of inspiration to her. The house was called Alderbury in *Five Little Pigs*. In that novel, the battery garden is also mentioned. *Ordeal by Innocence* opens with Dr. Calgary's driver taking him down the hill to the quay, where he boards the ferry to cross the river. In the short story "The Shadow on the Glass" in *The Mysterious Mr. Quin*, a secret passage similar to one at Greenway features in the story.

Throughout her life, Agatha Christie collected homes the way other people collect stamps. She loved buying them, decorating them, and working in their gardens. In addition to Greenway, Ashfield, Christie's childhood home, provided fodder for her writing.

In *Postern of Fate*, several scenes revolve around the greenhouse, called Kai Kai, which is based on the greenhouse of the same name at Ashfield. In both the real and fictional homes, the old greenhouse was used for the storage of abandoned toys and sports equipment. In *Postern of Fate*, several of the items found in Kai Kai hold important clues to the mystery, such as the Truelove, a cart and horse named after Agatha's childhood cart and horse. There's also a monkey puzzle tree mentioned in *Postern of Fate*. This unusual tree was grown at Ashfield, and one is still growing today at Greenway.

Christie's love of gardening is readily apparent in her novels, especially the later ones, in which she confidently describes shrubbery and herbaceous borders. As they age, her characters, notably Miss Marple, lament the fact that they can't garden any more, reflecting Christie's own frustration, but their love of gardening remains. In *Nemesis*, Jane Marple traps two women in their pretence at being knowledgeable gardeners. Miss Marple's knowledge of the rampant habit of the plant Polygonum baldschuanicum also leads her to deduce the location of a victim's body.

Mention Agatha Christie, and many readers picture the quintessential English village, but it's not just houses and gardens that inspired the best-selling mystery writer of all time (over two billion books sold, and still selling). It's also the social landscape. In Christie's fictional world, all is not as it seems. It's the tensions below the surface that frequently provide the clues to solving the mystery.

St. Mary Mead, for example, is complete with vicarage, elderly ladies knitting over afternoon tea, and charming cottage gardens. Hidden behind the hydrangea, however, is an unlikely heroine. Miss Marple's field glasses are trained not on the birds but on the mysterious new neighbors. The elderly ladies' seemingly innocent tea time provides essential gossip about the servant situation in the village. Best of all, there's a murder at the vicarage.

From small village to bustling London, from mysterious strangers to the pillar of the community, to the servant who knows everything about the family, Agatha Christie nails her characterizations on the head every time, and it's largely due to the way she was raised.

Agatha Miller was born on September 15, 1890, the last of three children, to an English mother and an American father. It was from her mother, perhaps, that Agatha inherited her love of houses. Before Agatha was born, her father was on a trip to America when her mother impulsively bought Ashfield, a large home in the Devon resort town of Torquay. Although her parents had initially planned to move to America, they loved Torquay so much that they decided to stay there. It was at Ashfield that Agatha was born and raised. Her childhood home was so important to her that when her father died and her mother began having financial difficulties, Agatha's writing income provided the crucial means in helping to keep the house.

Her mother taught Agatha to respect servants and their expertise. This respect would later be reflected in the characters of Hercule Poirot and Miss Marple. In virtually all of the novels these characters appear in, both detectives glean important clues from chats with the servants. They value servants in a way the official police rarely do.

Agatha was educated at home, and her mother encouraged her to have a lively curiosity. From an early age, Agatha loved literature and enjoyed making up her own stories. When Agatha complained about being confined to bed during an illness, her mother encouraged her to write a story. She did, and went on to write several other short stories and one novel called *Snow in the Desert*. None were accepted by publishers. Later, Agatha amusingly attributed the title *Snow in the Desert* to one of the characters, a writer, in her book *Death on the Nile*.

One day, Agatha told her sister, Madge, that she was thinking of writing a detective story. Madge replied that it would be very difficult and bet Agatha she couldn't do it. Agatha, of course, decided that she *would* do it. It wasn't until her first husband, Archibald Christie, was away fighting in World War I, however, that Christie finally sat down to write that detective story. Drawing on her work in a hospital dispensary, Christie centered her mystery on poisons. Belgian refugees were living near Ashfield, prompting Christie to make her detective, Hercule Poirot, a Belgian. *The Mysterious Affair at Styles* was published in 1920, launching a phenomenal career.

As Christie's career rose, however, her marriage began to decline. It ended in divorce, leaving her with a young daughter. Her writing career continued to flourish, and after a few years, romance came again. In 1930, Agatha married archeologist Max Mallowan.

Christie accompanied her second husband on his archeological digs, where she continued to write but also helped with the scientific work, photographing and cleaning antiquities. The couple divided their time between a house in Wallingford, near Oxford, and the house in Devon known as Greenway.

Just as her mother had impulsively bought Ashfield, Christie bought Greenway. She had actually visited the house with her mother when she was a child, and her mother had always said it was a perfect house. When Christie bought the house in 1938, however, it was in a bad state of repair. She and Max began renovating it extensively. Unfortunately, World War II intervened.

Anxious to help in whatever way possible, Christie offered the house for the use of evacuees. The garden was given over to vegetable gardening. Christie went to live in London while Max went off to war. At one point, the Admiralty requisitioned Greenway as an officer's mess for the American navy. They left behind a fresco that a naval officer painted in the library. It depicts the house nestled among the trees above the river. After the war, Christie returned to Greenway and decided to keep the fresco as a memento of the house's use during the war.

The house was turned over to Christie's daughter, Rosalind, and her husband, Anthony Hicks, in 1959. At first, Rosalind and Anthony lived in the Ferry Cottage. They moved into the main house in 1967. Anthony began a nursery garden business, and they bought an adjoining 270 acres called Lower Greenway Farm.

Christie died on January 12, 1976. She's buried in the village of Cholsey, near her home in Wallingford. She had requested that the following passage from Spenser, which Mrs. Folliat, the former owner of Nasse House in *Dead Man's Folly* quoted, be placed on her tombstone:

Sleepe after toyle, Port after stormie seas.
Ease after warre, Deathe after life does greatly please.

VISITING GREENWWAY

Administered by the National Trust.

Greenway Road

Galmpton, nr Brixham, Devon TQ5 0ES

Phone: (0)1803 842382

www.nationaltrust.org.uk/greenway

Large gift shop.

Hours: Early March to October 30, Wednesdays through Saturdays, 10:30 a.m.–5:00 p.m.

Open also on Tuesdays in April and August; 10:30 a.m.–5:00 p.m.

Admission: adults £9.75 pounds, concessions to children and families

Discounts for groups and for those arriving by "green ways"

Free to members of the National Trust.

Garden tours in the afternoon: extra charge

Wheelchair access: Disabled parking is available closer to the house than the main car park. There are many steep and slippery paths on the grounds, so the areas around Visitor Reception are the most accessible to those in wheelchairs.

Accessible toilets are next to Visitor Reception. The café is accessible. Braille and large-print guides are available.

The house and gardens are both open to the public and operated on a timed-ticket system—only 20 people in the house at a time. Buy your ticket first, then you can explore the gardens, barn gallery, and gift shop while waiting for entry to the house.

Extremely limited parking is available—you MUST book a parking space in advance, either by phone or through the web site.

The garden:

Christie loved roses, and Rosalind planted an "Agatha Christie Rose" on the Greenway grounds to honor the anniversary of her mother's 100th birthday. Rosalind turned the gardens over to the National Trust in 2000.

There have probably been gardens on the Greenway estate for at least 400 years. The location on a steeply sloping riverbank means it has excellent drainage and therefore little frost damage. Also, the temperature in the area rarely falls below freezing, accounting for the success of subtropical plants such as camellias and a wide variety of magnolias and rhododendrons. Many of the camellias in the present garden are more than 100 years old.

Begin a visit to these historic gardens at Visitor Reception, a building that dates back to the 1700s. When you take the guided tour with the gardener (highly recommended), this is where he or she will start the tour.

Whether guided or on your own, you'll probably start your tour with a look at the tennis court. It's called a Tennis Quick court, one of the first all-weather courts. Max Mallowan planted a Magnolia campbellii near the entrance and waited anxiously for it to bloom. It took 20 years.

Max especially liked wildflowers, and he kept a list of those in the garden, noting when they bloomed each year. Primroses, violets, bluebells, campions, and foxgloves, along with naturalized plantings of daffodils and cyclamen, are still featured today.

Next, wander into the South Walled Garden. This was where Anthony Hicks's nursery was located. Recently, a 19th-century glasshouse called a vinery has been renovated.

Head south across the lawn and turn left into the North Walled Garden. Here is the current working nursery garden, where plants from the estate are being propagated. Most days, there are plants available for sale at Visitor Reception. If you want a plant grown specifically at Greenway, however, be sure and ask about it, as some of the plants for sale are propagated from other National Trust properties.

From the nursery garden, walk out onto the Putting Green, where the family played a game called Clock Golf. A hole would be cut in the middle of the lawn. Then 12 starting points would be placed in a circle around the target hole, rather like numbers on a clock. Participants would then hit a golf ball from each of the 12 points. The one sinking the most putts was the winner.

In the spring, visitors will find hellebores blooming here. The dahlias bordering the Putting Green are said to have been planted by Agatha Christie and haven't been lifted since then. They provide a glorious riot of color in the summer and fall. The view beyond the dahlias provides a brief glimpse of the house.

The Fernery is, naturally, heavily wooded, providing a cool, shady respite from a hot summer day. It features a rustic water garden and is bordered by a pet cemetery for the family dogs.

The Hydrangea Walk leads away from the Fernery and, in addition to hydrangeas, also has spring-blooming rhododendrons. The walk opens onto a wonderful view of the house. Christie's autobiography features a photo of her and Max standing in almost this exact spot.

Following the path to the right, past the monkey puzzle tree, is a reclining sculpture called *Mother and Child* by local artist Bridget McCrumm. This piece, and several others placed throughout the garden, was donated to the National Trust from Rosalind Hicks's personal collection.

At this point, the pathways become rather steep and can be slippery when wet. Those who are willing to venture forth will be rewarded by wonderful views of the River Dart, along with woodland wildflowers, camellias, and magnolias.

The main path leads down to the river and the boathouse featured in *Dead Man's Folly*. The current structure wasn't built until the early 1800s, but an earlier version was known locally as Raleigh's Boathouse because Sir Walter Raleigh liked to sit there and smoke his pipe. Raleigh was half-brother to Sir Humphrey Gilbert, son of one of the early owners of Greenway, and he therefore visited often. Legend has it that one day a servant saw the smoke from Raleigh's pipe and thought Raleigh was on fire and threw water on him.

The bottom level of the boathouse contains a bathing pool. When the tide comes up the River Dart, salt water floods this room. Owners of the property from Georgian times to the present bathed here, believing salt water to be therapeutic.

The second level of the boathouse, reached by stairs in the back of the building, consists of one large room with two fireplaces and some of Christie's own rattan furniture. A balcony looks out over the river. If you're on a guided tour, ask the gardener to point out the house of Bridget McCrumm, the sculptor whose work is featured in the garden.

Heading back uphill through the woods, you'll come across a variety of crumbling walls, sculptures, water features, and wildflowers. In spring, the Camellia Garden rewards the visitor with glorious blooms.

The path leads past the house to the Stable Block. What better way to finish a visit to this historic, glorious garden than with afternoon tea at the Barn Café?

The house:

I'm sorry to report that the house wasn't open when I visited, so I can't give a first-hand account of what you'll find there. However, here are a few notes on what you can expect. After an introductory talk by a steward, you'll be free to wander the house on your own.

The emphasis is on the fact that this was Agatha Christie's holiday home – she didn't do any actual writing here. It's a family home filled with personal items and represents a way of English family life that was typical in the 1950's. Christie's grandson, Mathew Prichard, donated over 5,000 items that the family collected over many years. Some of the collections include china, wooden boxes, silver, and – of course – books. There's a complete collection of all of Christie's works.

Christie's grand piano is in the drawing room. It was here that she would read her novels to family and friends. She says in her autobiography that Max always guessed the killer before she got to the end and he was always right.

The library was Christie's favorite room. Here you'll find the frieze created by the U.S. navy while they occupied the house during WWII.

Christie's manual Remington typewriter, which used to be on display at Torre Abbey, is now at Greenway. She used it to type up her manuscripts, even when traveling on archeological expeditions with her husband Max Mallowan. Handwritten notes show Christie's spidery handwriting. Notebooks reveal the cryptic notes she made to herself about plots and characters.

Years later, even Christie had trouble following her train of thought when reviewing these notebooks.

Christie's bedroom displays her luggage and clothing, as though she's just left for a moment, but is about to return at any moment and pack for a trip.

Interactive displays throughout the house explore writing and archeology. You'll also hear recordings of Christie's own voice, dictating notes for her autobiography.

GETTING THERE

The National Trust is required to restrict the number of visitors' vehicles using the local roads, so those planning to arrive by car **must** reserve a parking space two days in advance. Large buses are not permitted. The largest size allowed is a mini coach with a 25-seat maximum.

By train: Take a mainline train to Paignton and then take the scenic steam railway (across from the Paignton train station) to Churston. Then take a taxi to Greenway.

A very scenic but more time-consuming route is to take the steam railway from Paignton to Kingswear, then take the ferry across the river to Dartmouth and then take the ferry up the River Dart, as described below. Although this doesn't look like a long trip on a map, it takes a lot of time, given the limited departure times of the steam railway and the ferries. If going this route, leave Paignton early in the morning.

By car: From the A379, take the left turn onto Kennel Lane, then left, following the signs for Greenway Ferry. Then left into the Greenway Estate car park. It's a short walk from there to Visitor Reception.

By ferry: This is by far the easiest, most scenic, and traditional approach. Catch the ferry in Dartmouth at the booking office near the end of the South Embankment, directly opposite the yellow Harbour Office. On Wednesdays through Saturdays, the 30-minute trip leaves Dartmouth four times a day, starting at 10:30 a.m., and returns from Greenway Quay four times a day. Be sure to tell the captain which return boat you expect to take, as they sometimes skip the last trip of the day if they're not expecting anyone to be leaving Greenway at that time. See (www.riverlink.co.uk) or (www.greenwayferry.co.uk)

for more information.

On the way up the river, you'll have a great opportunity to photograph the Greenway Boathouse on the right and also the picturesque Ferry Cottage. From the Greenway Quay, it's a *steep* uphill walk about 800 yards to the entrance. On the way, you'll pass the Lodge, one of two holiday rentals on the grounds. Book one of them through the National Trust www.nationatrustcottages.co.uk.

PLACES TO EAT

The Barn Café at Greenway has excellent, freshly prepared food using local produce.

WORKS BY AGATHA CHRISTIE

Because Christie published more than 80 novels and short story collections, plus plays and nonfiction works, only the highlights are mentioned here:

Mysterious Affair at Styles—1920 (Published in America first, then in England in 1921, this is Christie's first published book and Poirot's first case.)

The Secret Adversary—1922 (Tommy and Tuppence Beresford's first case)

Murder of Roger Ackroyd—1926 (considered one of her best, and most controversial)

Murder at the Vicarage—1930 (Miss Marple's first case)

Giant's Bread—1930 (first book published under the pseudonym Mary Westmacott)

And Then There Were None (book)—1939 (Christie considered this the best thing she ever wrote.)

And Then There Were None (play)—1943 (revived in London, 2005)

Come, Tell Me How You Live—1946 (For those who prefer nonfiction, this is Christie's account of life with her husband Max Mallowan during his archeological digs in the 1930s. It begins with a humorous poem describing her first meeting with Max.)

The Mousetrap (This play opened November 25, 1952, at the Ambassadors Theatre, starring Richard Attenborough and

Sheila Sim. It is still running, currently at St. Martin's Theatre in London. It's the longest continuously running play in the world.)

Star over Bethlehem—1965 (poems and short stories, including a thought-provoking version of the birth of Jesus)

Postern of Fate—1973 (the last novel Christie wrote)

Curtain—1975 (Poirot's last case)

Sleeping Murder—1976 (Miss Marple's last case)

(*Sleeping Murder* and *Curtain* were actually written during World War II and kept in a vault to be published after Christie's death; however, only *Sleeping Murder* was actually published after her death. *Curtain* was published a month before.)

RELATED SITES TO VISIT

Torquay Museum (www.torquaymuseum.org then click on Agatha Christie Gallery): The Agatha Christie Gallery at the Torquay Museum chronicles Christie's life and work. Start with the poisons exhibit, which describes her background as a dispensary assistant. Also of interest is the Poirot display, which features costumes worn by David Suchet in the BBC production of the Poirot stories. The Miss Marple section features costumes worn by Joan Hickson in the BBC production of the Miss Marple stories. On display also is the letter written to Joan Hickson by Agatha Christie. In it, Christie expresses her hope that Hickson would one day play Miss Marple.

Stop for afternoon tea at the nearby **Imperial Hotel in Torquay**. The last scene of Miss Marple's last case, *Sleeping Murder*, is set on the terrace of this hotel. The Imperial is also where Poirot and Hastings stay in *The Body in the Library*, although it's named the Majestic Hotel in that book.

Torre Abbey (www.torre-abbey.org.uk): This former monastery is now a museum and the garden features the Agatha Christie Potent Plants section. It features plants that were medicinal or poisonous, many of which were used in Christie's stories. Four beds in this garden have been planted to represent four Christie stories that featured poisonous plants in the plot. Visitors are encouraged to exercise their "little grey cells" and figure out which story each bed represents.

Brown's Hotel, Albemarle Street, Mayfair, London (www.brownshotel.com): Luxury hotel that is widely known to be the inspiration for *At Bertram's Hotel*. An Agatha Christie plaque can be seen in the lobby. Book afternoon tea there and soak up the old world atmosphere. Phone (0)20 7493 6020. Nearest Underground stop is Green Park on the Piccadilly, Jubilee, or Victoria lines.

ARMCHAIR TRAVELING

www.agathachristie.com is a Christie fan site.

www.poirot.us is a Hercule Poirot fan site.

www.christiemystery.co.uk is an exploration of Christie's writing.

www.orient-express.com is where you can book a trip on the luxury train.

www.englishriviera.co.uk has information on the annual Agatha Christie Festival held in Torquay.

FURTHER READING

An Autobiography by Agatha Christie. (This book was started in 1950, finished in 1965, but not published until 1977, the year after Christie's death. This is her life in her own words, although the original manuscript was edited by her daughter before publication.)

The Life and Crimes of Agatha Christie by Charles Osborne, 1982. (This is an interesting presentation of Christie's works in order of their writing, along with short descriptions of what was happening in Christie's life at the time she wrote them.)

Agatha Christie: A Biography by Janet Morgan, 1984. (Authorized by the family, this work fleshes out Christie's autobiography.)

Agatha Christie's Secret Notebooks by John Curran, 2009. Fascinating insight into Christie's writing methods, taken directly from her recently discovered notebooks.

taxi Cheng 1 800 487-7738

CPSIA information can be obtained
at www.ICGtesting.com
Printed in the USA
LVXC02n2258221115
463714LV00001B/1

* 9 7 8 1 4 5 7 5 0 2 4 6 0 *